STIGMATA

Also by Ian Wilson

Exodus
Jesus: The Evidence

STIGMATA

An Investigation into the Mysterious Appearance of Christ's Wounds in Hundreds of People from Medieval Italy to Modern America

Ian Wilson

1817

Harper & Row, Publishers, San Francisco
New York, Grand Rapids, Philadelphia, St. Louis
London, Singapore, Sydney, Tokyo

Illustration Acknowledgments

The photographs in this book are reproduced by kind permission of the following:

The British Museum, 6 bottom; Mary Evans Picture Library, 7; The Mansell Collection, 1, 6 above; Our Lady of Grace Capuchin Friary, San Giovanni Rotondo, Italy, 3; Pix Features/Stern, 5; TV South, 4

The remaining photographs come from the author's collection.

STIGMATA. Copyright © 1989 by Ian Wilson. All rights reserved. Printed in the United States of America. No part of this book may be used or reproduced in any manner whatsoever without written permission except in the case of brief quotations embodied in critical articles and reviews. For information address Harper & Row, Publishers, Inc., 10 East 53rd Street, New York, NY 10022.

FIRST U.S. EDITION

Library of Congress Cataloging-in-Publication Data

Wilson, Ian, 1941–
    Stigmata: an investigation into the mysterious appearance of
  Christ's wounds in hundreds of people from Medieval Italy to modern
  America / Ian Wilson.–1st U.S. ed.
     p.   cm.
    Includes index.
    Bibliography: p.
    ISBN 0-06-250974-8
    1. Stigmatization.   I. Title
BV5091.S7W55   1989
248.2'9 – dc19   88-43270
                                                     CIP

89   90   91   92   93   RRD   10   9   8   7   6   5   4   3   2   1

A miracle does not happen
in contradiction to nature,
but in contradiction to that
which is known to us of nature

St Augustine *De civitate Dei*, XXI, 8

CONTENTS

AUTHOR'S PREFACE

MY interest in stigmata goes back many years, and is a direct result of my long-term interest in the Turin Shroud, the cloth reputed to have been the original burial cloth of Jesus, imprinted with his image and wounds.

Stigmatics are professed to bear on their bodies replications of the crucifixion injuries suffered by Jesus, and an inevitable early question I needed to face was whether their wounds differed from, or were similar to, those indicated on the Shroud. Since the answer was, for the most part, the former, this raised the problem: why, and in particular, how are stigmata to be explained and understood in our twentieth century.

In the event the quest for that understanding has been as problematic as any mystery I have tackled. The geography of stigmatics is world-wide, the file of their case histories spans more than seven centuries, and not least, in the extensive literature about them they have all too frequently been approached from a rose-tinted religious viewpoint, rather than from the serious medical and psychiatric angle.

Indeed that literature is so vast, and so much of it locked in languages such as Latin and Italian, neither of which I read with any fluency, that it is only right that I acknowledge my indebtedness to the scholarship of some particularly valuable English language secondary sources, not least, ironically, the writings of one man who in his time was most damning on the Shroud's authenticity, Jesuit theologian the Revd Herbert Thurston. Thurston's *The Physical Phenomena of Mysticism*, posthumously published in 1952, ranges far beyond the phenomenon of stigmata, yet remains one of the most definitive books available on the subject, along with Montague Summers' lesser work of the same title published two years previously. I have also greatly valued, and found need for frequent reference to, René Biot's *The Riddle of the Stigmata*, published in translation from the original French in 1962.

Clearly desirable for a work of this kind (although Biot managed without it) has been access to a living stigmatic, in which context I have particularly valued the help accorded to me by Jane Hunt of Derbyshire, her husband Gordon, her former vicar, the Revd Norman Hill of Walsingham, and not least, BBC broadcaster and writer Ted Harrison, who first brought Jane's existence to my attention.

Among the many others deserving of my thanks should be mentioned Antonio Menna of Rome, who looked out for me press stories on some of the living Italian stigmatics; the Marquis and Marchioness of Lothian, who generously helped me with enquiries into the case of English stigmatic Teresa Higginson; Canon John Smith of Bristol for introducing me to the literature on English stigmatic Dorothy Kerin; the librarian of the Farm Street Church for making available the particularly rare pamphlet by Dr Alfred Lechler on his case of Elizabeth K.; Mrs Iris Sampson of Backwell, Bristol, for kindly translating this pamphlet from the German; the Central and University libraries of Bristol; and not least my editor and publisher, David Roberts, who encouraged me at every stage, and, when a spell of ill-health hindered the book's progress, generously allowed me to exceed the originally agreed deadline.

In order to help the reader trying to keep track of intermittent mentions of a bewildering welter of stigmatics, I have resorted to certain simplifications. For instance, some of the German stigmatic Therese Neumann's biographers have referred to her by the diminutive 'Resl', by which her family and close friends knew her. Others have adopted variant spellings of her Christian name, e.g. Theresa. For consistency, even when directly quoting from other books, I have referred to her, according to the most common usage, as Therese.

For similar reasons, rather than laboriously relate background details for each stigmatic mentioned in the text, I have provided as an appendix what amounts to a dictionary of stigmatics' biographies, initially compiled as much for my own working reference as for the reader's. Although this suffers from the minor disadvantage of being arranged in chronological rather than alphabetical order, the century in which each stigmatic lived is almost invariably quoted in the main text, and the arrangement has the advantage that each stigmatic can be better seen in his or her historical context.

Bristol, England   Ian Wilson

INTRODUCTION

NO-ONE knows what we call our mind – as distinct from our brain – actually is, or even if it is. Yet there can be no doubt that the thoughts and images that come into our mind can have rapid and readily demonstrable physical effects. A shock or unexpected revelation of some guilty secret from the past may make us turn white. Fear may give us goose-pimples, or cause us to break out in a cold sweat. An insulting remark can turn our whole complexion – if we are white-skinned – crimson with anger. The reading of a sexually explicit novel may make us blush pink with embarrassment. In a male, the viewing of a provocative striptease may cause an erection. Our skin, indeed our whole flesh, is clearly a mirror of our mind, and in so many of these instances it is our blood supply that has been affected, often in a very localised way.

Now, while we like to suppose that some imaginary 'I' living inside our brain-space is actually in charge of our bodies, the particular feature of all the above-mentioned physical changes is that they occur quite independently of any conscious volition or control. Indeed, so far as our normal consciousness is concerned, they may be an embarrassment in themselves, providing to others too obvious a barometer of how we really feel. Yet if we ask what scientifically may be responsible for triggering such dramatic non-conscious reactions from within us, the answer is that no-one really has any idea. However much we may think we know about the exterior universe of space, our interior universes of body and mind, and how they interact, are altogether more mysterious.

All this has a great deal to do with the phenomenon of stigmata. For if the stigmatics' central claim is valid, that bloody manifestations of Christ's crucifixion wounds spontaneously break out on their bodies, then clearly there can be little more dramatic demonstration of the sheer power of the something within us we call mind over the physical matter of our flesh and blood. No longer is it a matter of importance only to the more superstitious and reactionary among Roman Catholics. Arguably it may be of much more universal significance, particularly for our understanding of the furthest reaches of the effect of mind upon body.

But why should we believe the stories of stigmatics? Are they not all too far-fetched and alien to our rationalist twentieth-century thinking? Certainly much of what we are about to explore may seem unfamiliar and difficult to accept. But all that is asked is that we approach everything we are about to encounter step by step, and with a genuinely open mind.

THE DAY THE MARKS CAME

FOR most people in England, Thursday 25 July 1985 was quite
unmemorable. It was warm and sunny. In the garden of Buck-
ingham Palace the Queen presented a new standard to her Yeo-
men of the Guard. Seemingly the most noteworthy events were
unruly John McEnroe being asked to resign from the Queen's
Tennis Club, and the disclosure from across the Atlantic that film
star Rock Hudson was dying from Aids.

Yet although it attracted no headlines, what happened that day
to Jane Hunt, a bus driver's wife living in a semi-detached house
in the unremarkable village of Codnor, Derbyshire, was almost
unique in English history, and certainly unique to her that day
among the entire population of the United Kingdom. She developed stigmata, the mysterious wounds of Christ's crucifixion.

Although Jane did not realise it at the time, the first signs had
begun the evening before, when on going to bed she had seemed
to see a face of Jesus on the pillow, and had then gone on to
dream about him overnight. The next day, the 25th, was the Feast
of St James, the patron saint of her local church, and that morning,
as she prepared her family's breakfast, her hands seemed to burn
and itch. She dismissed it as no more than a temporary irritation.

Then at about 10 am, as she was walking towards the gate to
go shopping, she was suddenly riven by pains as of thousands
of needles being driven through the middle of her hands. The
pain was so intense that she had to drop her shopping bags and
rush back inside where, as her husband and daughter watched
incredulously, blood began to well from unbroken skin in the

centre of her palms and pour along her fingers.

Jane was terrified, and had no idea what was happening to her. Because of childhood deafness, and her father moving from coal-mine to coal-mine, her education had been minimal. She readily confesses: 'I didn't even know what stigmata were, because I was that slow at things.'[1]

But she was a regular worshipper at Codnor's local church, and urged by a friend, at the earliest opportunity she showed the marks to her vicar, the now retired Revd Norman Hill. He vividly remembers her showing them to him as they walked to the vicarage for a cup of tea. And it was he who recognised that somehow Jane, a coal-miner's daughter and hitherto totally unremarkable member of his Anglican congregation, had joined the exclusive ranks of St Francis of Assisi and St Catherine of Genoa, who centuries before had also apparently miraculously produced wounds of Jesus' crucifixion on their bodies.

Jane was so embarrassed about her wounds that she tried to hide them by wearing gloves, and coats with over-long sleeves, even by sitting on them. But they went on for two years, clearly visible on both sides of her hands, and for a limited time in her feet, although varying in intensity day by day. That the wounds on the back of the hands internally joined those on the front seemed evident when, in his vicarage kitchen, Revd Hill held both hands up to the light, revealing the tissues to be distinctly transparent in the region of the wounds. Particularly around Easter and on special Sundays they could be very deep and sensitive, sometimes discharging as much as a pint of blood during a twenty-four hour period. At other times they might be quiescent, and appear as little more than a raised bluish area on the back of each hand, with a corresponding indentation in each palm. Although quite recently they dried up and disappeared following a hysterectomy operation – frustratingly, just before I was able to examine them for myself – there can be no doubt of their reality. They were recorded in close-up for a thirty-minute television programme *Just Jane*[2] as part of the Television South documentary series *The Human Factor* screened in 1986.

In that programme, during interviews with journalist Ted Harrison, Jane disclosed other changes that had happened following that fateful St James' Day. She had experienced more visions of Jesus:

During prayer . . . it happens I'm moved and I've visited

Bethlehem. I've visited Christ. I've felt him put his arms around me.

She also saw his mother Mary, these latter visions sometimes occurring in the corner of the living room even while she and husband Gordon had been watching television. Invariably Gordon was unable to see anything, yet as he matter-of-factly acknowledged, Jamie the pet dog behaved peculiarly on such occasions:

It's normally very, very quiet, and we might be watching TV, and I'll look across at her, and Jane's looking up into the corner. And I'll look down at the dog, and the dog's looking up into the corner. I turn round, and there's nothing. And I'll say 'Is there somebody there?' And she'll say 'Yes!'[3]

Also following the onset of the stigmata, Jane felt a hitherto unrecognised capacity for healing. Encouraged by Revd Hill and his successor the Revd Peter Wyatt, at certain special services at Codnor she has donned a nun-like white dress and headscarf and laid her hands on those who have come to her for healing. She has had some apparent successes, as she recalls:

A lady came to church in a wheelchair. She'd never been able to walk, and I just told her to stand up, and she walked down the aisle, fine.[4]

Revd Hill also attests to her helping the healing of abscesses in his leg, although these have partly returned.

Despite such extraordinary happenings, Jane is at pains to emphasise her ordinariness: 'I've got a husband, and a daughter to bring up. I still have the ups and downs, and crises of paying bills and goodness knows what else'.

Yet while she may be considered ordinary when compared with some of the 300 or so others among history's known stigmatics, many of whom had more spectacular and more permanent wounds and led more colourful lives, her importance is that she is of our own time, and, for those of us living in Britain, here within this country. Effectively she is living proof that a phenomenon often dismissed as a bizarre syndrome of long-dead Catholic neurotics is neither so remote nor so exclusively Catholic – for Jane is Anglican – as popularly supposed.

Accordingly she provides a benchmark of factuality against which at least something of the credible and incredible that has been written about the great stigmatics of the past may be assessed. Just what an extraordinary phenomenon we are dealing with is best exemplified by one of the most recent of the 'great' stigmatics, Italy's Padre Pio, who died at the age of eighty-one in 1968. Jane, as has already been noted, became stigmatised on a day of special significance for her, the Feast Day of St James. Not only is St James the patron saint of her church, she also appears to have named her pet dog after him. What happened to Padre Pio seems to have been associated with a similar special anniversary.

Padre Pio was born in 1887, the son of poor, devoutly Catholic, parents Orazio and Maria Forgione, living in the village of Pietrelcina on the outskirts of Naples. Christened Francesco, or Francis, the boy's patron saint was inevitably St Francis, and when with the encouragement of his parents he decided upon a religious vocation, it was the Franciscan order he chose. It was only after his ordination that he took on the name Padre Pio. Not long after his ordination, in September 1915, the week of the anniversary of St Francis of Assisi's stigmatisation, he happened to be temporarily back with his parents, praying in a little hut at the far end of their garden, when he came out waving his hands in the air as though they had been stung by bees. Just like Jane Hunt, he complained of needle-like pains. Then these faded and became all but forgotten.

But as events were to prove, they were only a curtain-raiser for what was to follow. Three years later Pio had become one of the Capuchin friars, the most austere branch of the Franciscan order, living at San Giovanni Rotondo, an impoverished village high up in the Gargano region that forms the spur of Italy's boot. On 20 September, 1918, the exact anniversary of the stinging pains incident, the friars had just finished celebrating Mass in their church high above the village, leaving Pio still on his knees in the choir, apparently deep in contemplation of a statuette of the Crucifixion. Perhaps significantly, this still extant statuette is a particularly graphic one, the hands and feet liberally covered with blood from the nails, the chest peppered with scourge marks, and the knees bloody and broken as if from repeated falls. Suddenly Pio screamed, shattering the silence and bringing his fellow friars running back into the church to his aid. Bending over his unconscious body, they saw blood pouring from what seemed to be deep nail-holes in his hands and feet. On lifting him up, more blood could be seen soaking through his habit from an apparent stab wound in his left chest. Yet there was no sign that he or anyone else had inflicted such injuries. And that there really was something peculiar about the wounds became clear from the fact that even long after he had regained consciousness they did not begin to heal. Throughout the entire subsequent fifty years and three days that remained of his life they stayed day and night, without remission. Repeatedly they would open, scab over and then bleed again, resisting every attempt to heal or cure them, yet never becoming infected.

Just as Jane nearly seventy years later tried to hide her wounds, so Padre Pio from the very outset was loath to have his affliction turn him into a public spectacle. Although he could not hide the wounds from his fellow friars – not least, the pain of the holes in his feet made him walk with a pronounced limp – he pleaded with them to keep his condition a secret.

But inevitably, the news leaked out, and by 19 June 1920 the story of Padre Pio had become a subject of discussion even at breakfast tables in Britain. As the *Daily Mail* of that day reported:

> Extraordinary scenes are being witnessed in Foggia [the nearest main town to San Giovanni Rotondo] from day to day. The peasants refuse to confess to any but the young friar or to receive Communion from another's hand, and in consequence the rest of the monastery is idle, while long queues besiege the young Franciscan and gaze in wonder at the markings on his hands [and] sandalled feet . . .

Whatever the origin of the wounds, there can be no doubt that Padre Pio had them, just as in the case of Jane Hunt. Independent and even downright suspicious medical specialists were sent to examine him, some reporting that the apparent nail indentations in his hands were so deep that the flesh seemed penetrated right through. According to Dr Luigi Romanelli di Bartella, who was called in by Padre Pio's Father Provincial:

> I have a conviction amounting to certitude that the wounds are not superficial. Pressing on the palm with the thumb, one has the impression of a void. When thus pressing, it has not been possible to feel whether the wounds were joined together, for strong pressure causes the subject intense pain. I repeated the painful experiment, however, several times, both morning and evening, and must admit that I always came to the same conclusion.[5]

According to the Father Provincial himself, who visited Pio very shortly after the drama of 20 September:

> If I was interrogated by superior authorities on this particular question, I would have to answer and confirm under oath, so much is the certitude of the impression received, that, fixing one's glance on the wounds in the palms of his hands, it would be easy to recognise in its details written matter of an object previously placed on the opposite side, or back of the hands.[6]

An equally curious feature of the hand wounds, and notable also on Jane Hunt, was the fact that the immediately surrounding skin was quite clear and unblemished, with no sign of the sort of chafing and inflammation that might have been expected from anything self-inflicted. There are also many living individuals who directly witnessed Padre Pio's bleedings, including Roman Catholic Conservative Lord St John Fawsley, a former member of Prime Minister Margaret Thatcher's Cabinet.[7] Also official medical photographs of Padre Pio's hands, feet and side were taken early after the onset of Padre Pio's stigmatisation, and although these are well nigh inaccessible within the Vatican archives, many more unofficial ones exist, including colour photographs from his last years.[8]

But just as in the case of Jane Hunt, it was not only the strange bleedings that caused Padre Pio, in the teeth of every difficulty imposed by the Catholic Church, to become the subject of intense public interest. Whether or not he received visions is not known, because in a manner that may cause disbelief to non-Catholics, subsequent to his stigmatisation the Roman Catholic Church prohibited him from either writing anything publicly of his experiences, or from giving press interviews. If he ever wrote anything of this kind it will have been secreted within his file in the Vatican. Anything verbal has either died or will die with his confessors.

But the stories are legion of Padre Pio's powers of healing, as are reports of him mysteriously appearing all over Europe to individuals in need, despite his never physically having left San Giovanni Rotondo. One of the spectacular cures attributed to him was that of a little girl called Gemma Di Giorgi from Ribera in Sicily, apparently born without pupils in her eyes, and declared incurably blind by all the doctors who examined her. In 1947 Gemma was taken to San Giovanni Rotondo by her grandmother, and from the midst of the crowd attending the Mass was called by name to the altar by Padre Pio, and there told she must make her first Communion. After hearing her confession he stroked her eyes with his hand, and gave her Communion. When afterwards her grandmother asked if she had begged any favour from him, she responded that in all the excitement she had forgotten to make any such request. But later Padre Pio sought them out, and on his pronouncing words of blessing, suddenly Gemma cried out that she could see, a cure reputedly permanent and complete, despite the fact that she remained without pupils.[9]

If, as is likely, our immediate reaction to such stories is one of a healthy scepticism, it needs to be recognised that the Roman Catholic Church, far from vaunting Padre Pio as miracle worker, adopted a similarly critical attitude, and took the strongest measures to discourage the development of any cult around him, particularly during the first ten years after his stigmatisation. On 5 July 1923, the Sacred Congregation of the Holy Office in its official *Acta Apostolicae Sedis* pronounced that 'the happenings associated with the name of the devout Capuchin Padre Pio ... have not been proved to be supernatural in origin',[10] and followed this up in 1926[11] and 1931[12] with declarations that certain books written about Padre Pio were banned. The faithful were prohibited from visiting him, and even corresponding with him. He was debarred from hearing confessions. He was forbidden to conduct any public Mass. There was even an attempt to remove him from San Giovanni Rotondo which was unsuccessful only because the local populace threatened to resist this with force.

Although in time some of the restrictions were eased, he was allowed to hold just one daily public Mass, at the ungodly hour of five in the morning, and to hear confessions at any time. Inevitably, repression bred increased enthusiasm. The early Mass time provided an almost clandestine thrill for the huge crowds who gathered in darkness to attend, while the queues for his confessions were so long that there was often a wait of several days. This was despite Padre Pio spending up to eighteen hours a day in the confession box, sometimes releasing individual penitents from the burden of their sins with just a few brusque words.

The questions about Padre Pio and Jane Hunt, are obvious. Here we have two individuals, one male, one female, one living, one recently dead, exhibiting a phenomenon that seems to belong to the Middle Ages rather than modern times, accompanied by stories that sound too tall to be true, yet have such a ring of consistency that we have to wonder whether there might be something to them. But what?

One thing is certain. Jane Hunt and Padre Pio, although rare among humanity's millions, are by no means alone. During the late nineteenth century, well before Padre Pio had manifested his wounds, an elderly French medical professor, Dr A. Imbert-Goubeyre, impressed by meeting the contemporary Belgian stigmatic Louise Lateau, had begun the first semi-definitive assemblage of all known stigmatics from the thirteenth century to his own time.[13] Although his list suffers from omissions and the inclusion of some cases of arguable validity, it comprises no less than 280 female and forty-one male stigmatics, an interesting seven-to-one proportion of women to men. It is indicative of the Catholic Church's attitude to those who appear to manifest bleeding wounds that only sixty-two of the list have been beatified or made saints, and almost invariably for qualities other than their stigmata. Also unsurprisingly, well over a third of Dr Imbert-Goubeyre's collection were Italians, with a further seventy French and forty-seven Spanish, followed by thirty-three Germans, fifteen Belgians, thirteen Portuguese, five Swiss, five Dutch, three Hungarians and one Peruvian. A very high proportion were cloistered priests or nuns who belonged to one or other of the great religious orders, in particular the Cistercians, the Franciscans and the Dominicans.

But what is important is that the phenomena associated with a great many of these individuals were so bizarre that their contemporaries felt obliged to write down all that they observed. These accounts often seem absurdly exaggerated and far-fetched, yet in the light of Jane Hunt and Padre Pio they may just possibly be a little less so than has often been supposed. Certainly, what is remarkable is a common core of persistent features associated with stigmatics which becomes apparent the more one becomes familiar with each individual case.

So just who were the forbears of Jane Hunt and Padre Pio, and what were their stories? Let us begin at the beginning, with that most engaging yet tortured of saints, Francis of Assisi.

HOW STIGMATA BEGAN

IN September 1224 Francis of Assisi was forty-two years old, and undergoing yet another protracted, self-imposed fast, one in honour of the angels of heaven, to whom he had a great devotion. Through the kindness of the wealthy Orlando, Count of Chiusi, he and a few chosen companions had been provided with some suitably spartan huts on Monte La Verna, part of the Count's lands, and here since August 15, the Feast of the Assumption, they had held a retreat, praying and meditating amid the beech and pine trees, overlooking a delightful vista of the River Arno, its surrounding plain, and distant mountains.

In the Middle Ages 14 September was celebrated as Holy Cross Day, and accordingly on this particular morning, more than four weeks into the retreat, Francis with characteristic piety emerged from his hut before dawn and knelt in prayer, concentrating all his thoughts on what it must have been like for Jesus to suffer his death on the cross. As described in the so-called *Fioretti* or 'Little Flowers' of his doings and sayings:

> He began to contemplate the Passion of Christ . . . and his fervour grew so strong within him that he became wholly transformed into Jesus through love and compassion.
> And on this same morning, while he was thus inflamed by this contemplation, he saw a seraph [a form of angel] with six shining, fiery wings descend from heaven. This seraph drew near to Saint Francis in swift flight, so that he could see him clearly and recognise that he had the form of a man crucified . . .

As Saint Francis gazed on him he was filled with great fear, and at the same time with great joy, sorrow and wonder. He felt great joy at the gracious face of Christ, who appeared to him so familiarly and looked on him so kindly; but seeing him nailed to the cross, he felt infinite sorrow and compassion ... Then after a long period of secret converse this marvellous vision faded, leaving ... in his body a wonderful image and imprint of the Passion of Christ. *For in the hands and feet of Saint Francis forthwith began to appear the marks of the nails in the same manner as he had seen them in the body of Jesus crucified* ...[1]

The *Fioretti* go on to record that, just like Padre Pio and Jane Hunt centuries later, Francis was reticent and embarrassed about what had happened to him. He apparently said nothing to his companions, but:

... they nevertheless noticed that he did not uncover his hands or feet, and that he could not set his feet to the ground. And finding that his habit and under-garment were stained with blood when they washed them, they knew for certain that he bore the image and likeness of Christ crucified imprinted on his hands and feet, as well as in his side.[2]

Now it is known that the *Fioretti*, though based on earlier documentation, were composed by a Tuscan Italian nearly 100 years after Francis's death, and an understandable first reaction might be therefore to dismiss the whole story as typical medieval superstition and nonsense. But Francis's stigmatisation cannot be brushed aside so lightly, not least because first-hand corroborations of it have survived from individuals who were his companions on the La Verna retreat. One such companion was Brother Leo, who succeeded Francis as head of the Franciscan order, from whom has survived, still preserved in Assisi's Convent of Friars Minor, a personally written note on the back of some verses of blessing which Francis himself appears to have composed and given to Leo shortly after his experience. According to Brother Leo's note:

Two years before his death Francis was fasting ... in La Verna ... and the hand of God was upon him. After the vision and the words of the seraph *and the imprinting of the stigmata of Christ on his body* he composed the praises of God which are written on the other side of this sheet ...[3]

In addition Brother Leo is known, on Francis's death, to have sent out the following message to all the new order's Provincials:

I announce to you great joy, even a new miracle. From the beginning of ages there has not been heard so great a wonder, save only in the Son of God . . . For, a long while before his death, our Father and Brother [St Francis] appeared crucified, bearing in his body the five wounds which are verily the stigmata of the Christ. For his hands and feet had as it were piercings made by nails fixed in from above and below, which laid open the scars and had the black appearance of nails; while his side appeared to have been lanced, and blood often trickled therefrom.[4]

Another of Francis's companions on the retreat, Brother Masseo, recorded how difficult it had been for Francis to walk after his stigmatisation, a donkey apparently having been needed to help him down from La Verna:

Our dearest father had decided to bid farewell to the holy mountain on September 30, 1224 . . . My Lord Orlando, the Count of Chiusi, had sent up the beast for him to ride on, since on account of the wounds in his feet he could no longer walk.[5]

Within four years of Francis's death, which was itself only two years after the stigmatisation, his biographer Thomas of Celano recorded how the wounds were apparent even on Francis's corpse, the wounds of the nails apparently even having the resemblance of real nails:

It was wonderful to see amid his hands and feet, not the prints of the nails but the nails themselves formed out of his flesh and retaining the blackness of iron.[6]

And there survive no less than two paintings[7] of Francis from within ten years of his death, both showing him with the stigmata. On the second of these, by Bonaventura Berlingheri and preserved at Pescia, there is even depicted the apparent nail feature remarked on by Thomas of Celano. This painting has been described by artist and writer N.H.J.Westlake:

The picture now at Pescia . . . is singular from the circumstance that one hand has been turned so as to show the inside and the formation of the point of the nail turned down, which form, it is asserted, the flesh assumed . . .[8]

13

There can be little doubt, then, that Francis somehow acquired on La Verna the wounds we now call stigmata. So far as can be determined, he was the first person in history to do so in an apparently spontaneous way. There is a suggestion that St Paul within a few decades of Jesus's lifetime, may have been similarly marked, for at the end of his Epistle to the Galatians he cryptically concludes:

> I want no more trouble from anybody after this; the marks [*stigmata* is the actual Greek word used] on my body are those of Jesus.
>
> [Galatians 6: 17]

But since in St Paul's time stigmata meant any form of disfiguration such as a scar or a tattoo, it is possible that he was speaking metaphorically of the many beatings he suffered in Jesus' name. And in any case a yawning gap of more than eleven hundred years separates St Paul's time from that of St Francis.

So the inevitable question arises: what could have been so special about St Francis that he should feature this bizarre manifestation? Was it a wholly miraculous gift from God? Was it something about the psychology of the man himself and his time? Or might it have been merely some clandestine form of self-mutilation?

It is important that we should know something of Francis's background, which is well recorded. Certainly he was what might be popularly described as an oddball. Unusually among stigmatics, he was born into comparatively well-to-do circumstances, the son of a self-made and ostentatiously successful Assisi cloth merchant, Pietro di Bernadone and his wife Pica. Growing up in a tall house not far from where Assisi's post office now stands, the young Francis dressed flashily, enjoyed high living, and became a popular member of the town's wealthier young rakes. So he might have continued, eventually taking over his father's business, but for the outbreak of a mini-war between Assisi and its neighbour Perugia, during which, on riding out to participate in an ill-judged attack on Perugia, he was captured and flung into prison.

He was a year thus confined, and this seems to have had a devastating effect on him. When he returned home he was certainly a changed man. For some while he was seriously ill with fevers, and although on recovery he tried to get back to his old ways, even temporarily joining a new knightly exploit, he was persuaded to turn back from this by the hearing of a mysterious voice. Soon stories of more and more strange behaviour on his part began to circulate. In one he was said to have given away all the fine clothes he had been wearing in exchange for those of a knight who had fallen on hard times and was nearly naked. In another he had been seen visiting the local leper house, fraternising with the inmates and even kissing the rotting hands of one.

Matters began to come to a head when one day while out in the country he happened to pause at a hill-top church, San Damiano, so run-down – even though its aged priest was still living next door – that the walls were crumbled and weeds were growing through the paving stones. Something moved Francis to enter and kneel before the altar. As he did so his eyes fastened on the painted wooden crucifix that hung above him. This typically Byzantine work, now preserved in Assisi's Basilica of St Clare, is so lacking in realism that it shows Jesus stretched on the cross with his eyes wide open as in life, even though the lance wound is already in his side. Yet in that moment, for Francis, the crucifix seemed to come to life, with Jesus speaking to him, pleading for him to repair his church that had fallen into such ruin.

Francis left the church, gave the old caretaker priest all the money in his pocket, and rode back to his father's stores in Assisi. There he took some of the best bales of cloth, sold these and his horse in nearby Foligno, and walked the ten miles back to San Damiano to hand over this substantial sum of money to the old priest, with whom he now stayed.

When Francis's father returned home to discover what his son had done he was furious. On learning Francis's whereabouts he rode out to San Damiano to try to retrieve what his son had given away, only to find that Francis, apparently forewarned, was nowhere in sight. After about a month in hiding Francis did quietly slip back to Assisi, but to everyone's distaste was unkempt, without the money he had taken, and dressed only in rags. He even began begging, whereupon the townspeople, as soon as they recognised him, derided him as *pazzo, pazzo* – quite, quite mad.

It was all more than the proud Pietro di Bernadone could stand, and after a series of choleric confrontations with his son, he decided that since it was to the Church that Francis had given so much of his money, it was to the Church that he should appeal for its return. Accordingly he asked Assisi's irascible and luxury-loving Bishop Guido to summon a special court so that the dispute between him and his son could be settled once and for all.

Francis was summoned to present himself on a chilly day in 1206 at the forecourt of Assisi's Episcopal Palace, fronting the still surviving Piazza Santa Maria Maggiore, for a public hearing before Bishop Guido and an unusually large and expectant assemblage of the Assisi populace. He appeared at the appointed hour, dressed in a manner befitting a cloth merchant's son, and carrying a bag of money which could only be that which he had given to the church at San Damiano. Since it seemed he was about to repent, Bishop Guido spoke to him kindly, urging him to return his father's wealth, as it had not been his to give away.

Francis stood up, handed over the bag of gold, and slipped through a side door. Moments later he returned with the clothes he had been wearing clutched in front of him. With extraordinary aplomb he announced to the assembly:

> Hear all of you, and understand. Until now I have called Pietro di Bernadone my father. But since I now intend to serve the Lord, I give back to him the money, about which he has been so angry, and all the clothes which I have had from him. I wish to say only 'Our father, which art in Heaven', not 'my father, Pietro di Bernadone'.[9]

Then, tossing the bundle of clothes at his father's feet, he stood in the middle of the courtyard stark naked, so embarrassing Bishop Guido that he rushed forward to cover him with his own rich cape (later retrieved and replaced with an old tunic).

It was an extraordinary moment, immortalised by Giotto and other artists, in which Francis in the most literal sense stripped himself of all remaining earthly ties, believing that only thus could he take up the new life of poverty and self-renunciation that he was sure was the true way of Christ.

But although all this conveys to us something of the intensity of Francis's spiritual fervour, and thereby something of his psychology, it still does not provide us with any clear lead for the origin of the stigmata, which in any case lay still eighteen years in the future. Francis went on to gather round him the companions in a life of poverty who would become the nucleus of the Franciscan Order. But still, what precisely could have triggered the extraordinary manifestation on Mount La Verna?

While at this stage of our study we can only guess at possible contributory factors, one element that certainly distinguished Francis from almost anyone who had gone before was the sheer intensity with which he took upon himself poverty and hardship in order to divorce himself from the luxury-loving materialism that he saw to be the canker bedevilling the Church of his time. Shunning every form of comfort, typical of the privations he set for himself and his disciples is this description we have of them wintering at Rivo Torto, near Assisi, shortly after the Order's formal establishment:

> On dark and rainy days, when the water drove in through the leaky roof of the shed and the earth floor was black and miry and cold for the bare feet to tread upon, they sat there in their coarse ragged gowns, seven or eight in number, and had nothing to eat all day – and there was no fire to warm them and no books to read.[10]

When Francis fasted, he did not simply forego a few luxuries. During one Lent spent on a small island in Lake Trasimeno he is said to have eaten only half a loaf of bread in the entire forty days. Even allowing for exaggeration, such dangerously protracted mortifications could only lower his resistance to infection, and although neither the nature of his Perugian imprisonment illness nor his subsequent ailments can be identified with certainty, quartan malaria – that is, a malaria with fevers recurring every three or four days – has been authoritatively suspected.[11]

Certainly some such illness, probably contracted in Italy, caused him to cut short an evangelising expedition to Morocco as early as 1214. Six years later, on his return from a trip to Egypt to try to convert the Moslems, he began suffering from what his biographers called the Egyptian eye sickness, so that he continually had great pain in his eyes. The following year he was reported as still not entirely free from quartan fever, and by 1224, the very year of his stigmatisation, his biographer St Bonaventure records:

> He began to suffer from diverse ailments so grievously that scarce one of his limbs was free from pain and sore suffering. At length by diverse sickness, prolonged and continuous, he was brought to such a point that his flesh was wasted away and only as it were the skin clove to his bones.[12]

So we need to think of Francis as in extremely poor physical shape at the time he set upon himself the added privations of the fast at La Verna, a fast in which he continued to shun most of the comforts Count Orlando tried to provide for him. So yet again we must face the question: does all this have any spiritual or psychological bearing on the outbreak of spontaneous, crucifixion-like wounds on his body? Or might he have simply gouged the wounds himself as an additional form of self-mortification in an endeavour to make himself more Christ-like?

Certainly it needs to be taken into account that, alongside a fascination in art and literature with the more lurid of Jesus' sufferings, there had developed in Francis's time a peculiarly medieval predilection for trying to recreate the crucifixion in a directly physical way, both via miracle plays and via exhibitionistic acts of self-mutilation. As far away as England several contemporary and near-contemporary chroniclers record a curious case, apparently dated 1222 – two years before Francis received his wounds – in which a young man was tried before the Council of Oxford for having, according to the *Dunstable Annals*:

> made himself out to be Christ and . . . perforated his hands and feet.[13]

As independently recorded by the near-contemporary chronicler Thomas Wykes, writing in the very monastery used by the Oxford Council, the young man:

> caused himself to be crucified . . . declaring that he was the Son of God and the Redeemer of the world. By the sentence of the Council he was incarcerated and . . . shut up for the rest of his life.[14]

From these and later mentions of the case in Augustinian friar John Capgrave's *Chronicle of England*,[15] it appears that the young man had had his hands and feet deliberately perforated, in the manner that ear-lobes are pierced for ear-rings, and that for purposes of fairground-style spectacle he arranged for himself to be nailed to a cross at any opportunity.

Given such a religious climate, it cannot yet be discounted that St Francis, not necessarily with any conscious deception on his part, might in some hunger-crazed state have similarly physically inflicted crucifixion wounds upon himself. Nor, given the obvious saintliness that resulted in his canonisation within two years of his death, can it be ruled out that the wounds may have been a genuine, miraculous gift from God.

However, there emerged literally hundreds of stigmatics between St Francis's death and our own time of Jane Hunt and Padre Pio. Could all of them, consciously or unconsciously, have indulged in self-mutilation? Could all of these have attained the heights of saintliness of St Francis? Or does the real answer to the manifestation of the wounds lie in something else – perhaps in some as yet poorly understood process relating to the stigmatics' peculiar psychology? With the benefit of the plentiful and detailed accounts of history's stigmatics, often written from viewpoints little less sceptical than our own, we can explore further.

STRANGE SAINTLINESS

ONE feature that begins to tell us at least something about the nature of the phenomenon we are dealing with, particularly after all the centuries in which there had been no stigmatics, is the speed with which they proliferated immediately following the news of Francis's stigmatisation.

According to Dr Imbert-Goubeyre's list, for instance, no less than thirty-one had emerged before the end of the thirteenth century. At least one of these may even conceivably have slightly preceded Francis himself. For as early as 1231 there is record of apparently stigmatic wounds being observed on the body of a Premonstratensian monk, the Blessed Dodo of Hascha in Frisia, who was killed when the wall of an old ruin fell on him. According to a Latin biography of the time:

> Now when he had been crushed to death under the stones
> ... they discovered that there were open wounds in his hands
> and in his feet and in his right side after the fashion of the
> five wounds of our Saviour.[1]

Since the Blessed Dodo is known to have been a very old man when he died, he may have borne the wounds on his body for some years before his death without anyone being aware of the fact, and therefore possibly even before St Francis himself, although this can be no more than speculation.

But quite positively, as early as 1237 apparently spontaneous stigmata appeared on a Dominican nun, the Blessed Helen of Veszprim. Yet again these began on a special anniversary, no less than the Feast of St Francis, which only nine years previously had been set as October 4 following Francis's speedy canonisation. According to a forthright memoir drawn up by the nuns of Blessed Helen's own convent community:

> We, the Sisters of the Convent of St Catharine of Veszprim, relate and place on record all that we have seen with our own eyes touching the Lady Helen, our Sister, and we cannot be mistaken nor err, because for many years we did live most familiarly in her company. She had wounds in both hands, and in her feet, and her breast was also wounded. The first wound was made in her right hand upon the night of the Feast of St. Francis . . . and for all that she resisted, crying out: 'Lord, refrain; do not this thing, my Lord and God.' In very sooth we heard her utter these words, although we did not see with whom she wrestled, nor unto whom she spoke. The second wound was made at noon, upon the Feast of the Holy Apostles Peter and Paul [29 June].[2]

Notable, and consistent with what is to follow, is the feature of Blessed Helen wrestling and talking as if to some invisible presence.

Although we otherwise know comparatively little about Blessed Helen, and the nuns' memoir is obscured by descriptions of her apparently miraculous production of flowers, thanks to a detailed account by Philip, Abbot of the great Cistercian Abbey of Clairvaux, we know considerably more about her near-contemporary, the Belgian Cistercian nun Elizabeth of Herkenrode, near Liège, who died around the year 1275.[3] Even more than Francis of Assisi, Elizabeth spent a great deal of time in trance-like states, apparently re-enacting Jesus's Passion every twenty-four hours, beginning with his arrest at early morning Matins and ending with his laying in the tomb at late evening Compline. During these performances, according to Abbot Philip, Elizabeth:

> at one and the same time represented the person of our Lord who was suffering and the persecutor or executioner who was tormenting, the person of our Lord while he submits himself, and of the persecutor while he pushes, drags, smites or threatens.[4]

Abbot Philip's observations have been succinctly summarised by the Revd Herbert Thurston:

> When Elizabeth was contemplating some stage of our Lord's

ignominious progress from one tribunal to another, catching hold of the bosom of her own dress with her right hand she would pull herself to the right and then with the left hand she would drag herself in the opposite direction. At another time, stretching out her arm and raising her fist threateningly, she would strike herself a violent blow on the jaw so that her whole body seemed to reel and totter under the impact; or again, while her feet remained planted and motionless, she would pull herself fiercely by the hair until her head struck the ground. Similarly, bending back all her fingers except an outstretched forefinger, she would aim it at her eyes as if she meant to gouge them out, while at other stages writhing, as it seemed, in agony upon the floor, she beat her head against the ground over and over again. But the most frequently recurring feature in this ill-usage of herself was the shower of blows which, when lying on her back in the trance state, she rained upon her breast with extraordinary force and violence.[5]

Although it might not be altogether surprising, given such self-abuse, Elizabeth was reportedly fully stigmatised, and was probably the first of many stigmatics (though not Padre Pio nor Jane Hunt) to feature wounds around the top of the head, as from a crown of thorns. Abbot Philip, who acknowledged himself to have been initially sceptical, made his own close examination of Elizabeth's hands, feet and side. Particularly importantly, because it is in direct contradiction of the crucial wounds having been self-inflicted, he insisted that with others present he had on several occasions personally observed the blood pouring from these. He also attested to witnessing bleeding from her eyes and from beneath her nails (the latter ostensibly because Jesus's arms had been too tightly bound).

If we look at another stigmatic of the late thirteenth century, Lukardis of Oberweimar, her activity, not dissimilar to that of Elizabeth of Herkenrode, appears to have been even more overtly masochistic. Lukardis's biographer, who seems to have known her well, and to have set his observations in writing shortly after her death, states:

With regard to the hammering in of the nails of Christ's cross, as she carried the memory of it inwardly in her heart so she represented it outwardly in action. For again and again with her middle finger she would strike violently the place of the wounds in each palm; and then at once drawing back her hand a couple of feet she delivered another fierce blow in the same spot, the tip of her finger seeming somehow to be pointed like a nail. Indeed, though it appeared a finger to sight and touch, neither flesh nor bone could be felt in it and those who had handled it declared that it had the hardness of a piece of metal. When she struck herself in that way there was a sound like the ring of a hammer falling on the head of a nail or on an anvil. On one occasion a person in authority, thinking this kind of blow was a sham or a mere trick, in order to find out the truth put his hand in the way. But when she had struck but once he hastily drew back his hand, declaring that if he had waited for a second blow he would have lost the use of it forever. With the same finger, at the hour of sext and again at none, the servant of God [i.e. Lukardis] used to strike herself violently on the breast where the wound came. The noise that she made was so great that it echoed through the whole convent, and so exactly did she keep to the hour of sext and none in this practice that the nuns found the sound more trustworthy than the clock . . . Furthermore it should be noted that the servant of God, before the stigmata appeared, endeavoured, out of her great longing, to open the places of the wounds in her feet by boring them, as it were, with her big toe . . .[6]

Somewhat reassuringly, given such bizarre behaviour, no churchman appears to have considered either Elizabeth of Herkenrode or Lukardis of Oberweimar sufficiently saintly to press for their canonisation.

But in deference to Lukardis, her biographer in all openness pointed out that she had been boring away at herself in such a way for two years before the stigmata manifested themselves, and that when they did, the apparent trigger was not these physical attacks but, as in the case of Jane Hunt, a nocturnal vision. Although Lukardis's vision was not claimed as of Christ, it was nonetheless of a delicate young man bearing the same crucifixion wounds, and effectively one and the same as he. Pressing his right hand against hers, this visitant apparently told her: 'I want you to suffer along with me'. The moment she consented, an appropriate nail-wound instantly formed on her right hand.

Also, like Jane Hunt, Padre Pio and St Francis, Lukardis was reticent about her wounds, covering them with a form of mittens, and being persuaded to display them only with reluctance. And

23

in a manner different from the stigmatics we have so far seen, but in common with many to follow, her wounds reportedly bled regularly on Fridays, but remained dry the rest of the week. This 'body clock' feature repeatedly recurs in well-observed cases, yet Lukardis was one of the first to exhibit it. It would therefore be presumptuous at this stage to assume conscious or unconscious self-mutilation.

But if this is the case, neither, it would seem, can genuine saintliness be inferred, not even on the part of those actually bestowed this honour, such as the extraordinary St Maria Maddalena de' Pazzi of the late sixteenth century.

Like St Francis, Maria Maddalena was born into a well-to-do, and in her case, noble family, her father having been Camillo Geri de' Pazzi, of the famous Pazzis of Florence. The Christian name her parents gave her at birth was Caterina, perhaps reminiscent of the much-revered St Catherine of Siena, and since they were devout Catholics and she was their only daughter, she seems to have discovered early on that a highly effective way of getting her own way was to profess a precocious interest in religious discussions and practices, and to use this to achieve a certain dominance.

Even before the age of ten Caterina adopted the habit of hiding herself in 'the most secret part of the house',[7] and there whipping and mortifying herself with an improvised crown of thorns and prickly belt. Although her mother discouraged her from such practices by insisting that she sleep with her, when at the age of ten Caterina received her first communion she swiftly followed this with a vow of perpetual virginity, even though this was not what her parents wanted for her.

Four years later, on her father becoming governor of Cortona in Tuscany, Caterina went for part of her education to a nearby convent, soon showing off her whippings to the nuns, and insisting on carrying out all the most degrading tasks. At sixteen, after fending off her parents' last-ditch attempts to dissuade her, she joined the Carmelite nunnery of Santa Maria degli Angeli in Florence, a year later taking her vows and the religious name Maria Maddalena (Mary Magdalen), a singularly apposite choice.

Shortly afterwards she began, like Elizabeth of Herkenrode, to lapse into strange trance states, often with such suddenness that if she was eating she might remain cataleptically fixed with the food raised to her mouth, or if she was washing clothes in winter her hands might remain rigidly in the water until it froze around

24

them. At other times she would bound and caper ecstatically, with extraordinary agility. But accompanying these states – and here we see the significance of the name Mary Magdalen – she affected an abandoned spiritual ardour with highly charged sexual overtones. Sometimes she would seize a statue of Jesus and, removing all the drapes and trappings, exclaim that she wanted him to be naked, to remind herself of him as a naked child. The word 'love' apparently caused her paroxysms of excitement, causing her to repeat, as if in sexual climax: 'O Lord, my God, it is enough, it is enough, it is too much, O Jesus ... O God of Love, no, I can never stop from crying of love ... O love, you are melting and dissolving my very being. You are consuming and killing me .... Oh come, come, and love, love ...'[8]

Such were the extremes of these ardours that she began breaking all the rules of her nunnery, vomiting any food except bread and water, and abandoning her prescribed habit, stockings and shoes in favour of going barefoot, wearing just a simple tunic. This was somewhat skimpy for her various antics, which included, like Elizabeth of Herkenrode, writhing on the floor and being hit by invisible blows. But even this single remaining garment she would sometimes tear off in order to roll herself on thorns, or give herself another savage whipping.

Amid all this, and as early as the age of nineteen, Maria Maddalena developed stigmata. Just as in the case of Jane Hunt, she and items with which she had been in contact became accredited with various healings, and other supernormal powers were claimed of her. From the above case-history It should be quite evident to any psychiatrist that she had become a florid, sadomasochistic neurotic. The British scholar the late Eric Dingwall, who made a special study of her, remarked[9] that the criteria by which she became elevated to sainthood in the seventeenth century would be unacceptable given the psychological insights of the twentieth century.

Yet we cannot be certain whether such women, who clearly had a penchant for injuring themselves, produced their stigmata by self-mutilation, or whether there may genuinely be some other factor involved. But anyone looking for evidence of cheating has only to look to two stigmatic cases of the sixteenth century, one of these another strange nun named Magdalena, to find his arguments apparently fully justified.

Of Spanish birth, Magdalena de la Cruz joined a convent in her late teens, and then began ecstasies, mortifications and abstinence from food. Soon she had apparently received the stigmata, attracting such great veneration from Spain's noble families, including the Empress Isabella, that it became fashionable for expectant mothers to send their awaited infant's nursery furniture and clothing for Magdalena's blessing. No-one found her out, although St Ignatius of Loyola, the founder of the Jesuits, apparently had his suspicions. But in 1543, when Magdalena became seriously ill, she seems to have been so frightened of after-life retribution that she confessed that for years she had been practising a variety of deceptions. After a two-year trial she received a stiff sentence from the Inquisition for her sins.

Of similar mould, and directly contemporary with Maria Maddalena de' Pazzi, seems to have been the Portuguese Dominican nun Sor Maria de la Visitacion, the 'holy nun of Lisbon'. Sor Maria's stigmata, which included hand and foot nail-wounds, a wound nearly an inch long in the side, and 'crown of thorns' punctures on her forehead, became so famous that in 1587 her blessing was sought by, and granted to, the naval commander of the Spanish Armada, the Marquis of Santa Cruz.

However, suspicions began to be aroused when one of Maria's sister nuns claimed that through a chink of the cell door she had seen Maria in the act of painting one of the nail-wounds onto her hand. Some months before the Armada's departure, an inquiry was set up, headed by an Italian, Father Luigi di Granada. But although he arrived in Sor Maria's cell armed with a bar of soap and full investigative powers, he appears to have made the mistake of chivalrously accepting Maria's plea that even the slightest touch to her wounds caused her intense pain. He accordingly passed her stigmata as genuine and miraculous merely on the basis of visual scrutiny.

But soon after the Armada's defeat, and the evident failure of Maria's blessing, fresh investigations were opened up, this time by the Inquisition who stood for no nonsense. When they arranged for Maria's wounds to be unceremoniously scrubbed, the paint was washed away and unblemished flesh was revealed beneath. According to the report that the Venetian Ambassador Lippomano sent back to his master, the Doge, in Venice:

> The nun of Portugal [i.e. Maria] who was universally held for
> a saint has been found out at last. The stigmata are proved
> to be artificial and the whole trick invented to gain credit in
> the world. She was induced to act thus by two friars of her

26

Order of St Dominic, with a view to being able some day to tell the King that unless he handed Portugal over to Don Antonio he would be damned forever, and with the further object of raising a rebellion against the King. The friars are in the prisons of the Inquisition, the nun in a convent awaiting sentence . . .[10]

From such cases the phenomenon might seem a case of conscious or unconscious fraud on the part of attention-seeking neurotics in holy orders, except that even after well-publicised cases such as Sor Maria's, stigmata still simply refused to go away.

Thus within fifty years of Sor Maria's condemnation there emerged at Loudun in France, as classically recounted in Aldous Huxley's *The Devils of Loudin*,[11] the extraordinary case of Soeur Jeanne des Anges, Prioress of Loudun's then brand-new Ursuline convent. Emanating from frustrated infatuation for Loudun's Protestant parson, Urbain Grandier, Soeur Jeanne and many of her nuns had to be exorcised of various devils, procedures which in 1635 became such a matter of public spectacle that they even attracted visitors from abroad. Among these were the English playwright Thomas Killigrew, then still in his youth, and his friend Walter Montague, son of the first Earl of Manchester, recently converted to Catholicism.

Prior to the Englishmen's arrival, and just after the expulsion of one of Soeur Jeanne's devils, a bloody cross had appeared on her forehead and remained there, plainly visible to all, for three weeks. But yet more strange was what Montague and Killigrew witnessed for themselves as an apparent battle of wills between Soeur Jeanne and another of her devils, Balaam, who had announced that if he had to depart he would leave his name permanently imprinted on her left hand. Soeur Jeanne apparently felt that if she had to be branded with any name at all it should be that of St Joseph. Whereupon, to the fascination of her observers, her body began to be wracked with typical stigmatic writhings and convulsions, accompanied by gross swelling of her stomach, breasts, and tongue. Then, as described by Killigrew:

I heard her, after she had given a start and a shriek that you would have thought had torn her to pieces, speak one word and that was 'Joseph'. At which all the priests started up and cried: 'That is the sign, look for the mark!' On which one, seeing her hold out her arm, looked for it. Mr Montague and myself did the same very earnestly; and on her hand I saw a colour rise, a little ruddy, and run for the length of an inch along her vein, and in that a great many red specks, which made a distinct word; and it was the same she spake, 'Joseph'.[12]

Along with the other witnesses, Killigrew signed an affidavit that this was indeed what occurred, and subsequently Soeur Jeanne went on to exhibit other names in the same manner, those of Jesus, Mary and François de Sales. As described by Aldous Huxley:

Bright red at their first appearance, these names tended to fade after a week or two, but were then renewed by Sister Jeanne's good angel. The process was repeated at irregular intervals from the winter of 1635 to St. John's Day, 1662. After that date the names disappeared completely.[13]

In Killigrew's time, as would be expected in our own, every form of rational explanation was sought. Among the suggestions were that Soeur Jeanne had etched the names onto her skin with acid, or traced them on with coloured starch. It was particularly noted that instead of the names being distributed on both hands, they were all crowded on to the left, where it would have been easier for a right-handed person to write them.

But we have Killigrew's assured statement that he actually saw the name 'Joseph' appear spontaneously. And we know also that this and the other names kept on appearing, because Soeur Jeanne was well recorded exhibiting them to innumerable distinguished visitors and crowds of common sightseers during a tour she went on as a 'walking relic' in the late 1630s. In Paris her hand was viewed by the King and his Queen, Anne of Austria, followed by most of the city's population, who queued to view it while Soeur Jeanne sat in a ground floor room of the Hôtel de Laubardemont, dangling it out of the window from four in the morning until ten at night. As she subsequently complained in her journal:

I was given no leisure to hear Mass or to eat my meals. The weather was very hot and the crowd so increased the heat that my head began to swim and I finally fell in a faint on the floor.[14]

In less crowded circumstances the great Cardinal Richelieu examined the hand, vetoing a suggestion that it should be cased in a special sealed glove on the grounds that such a procedure would be testing God. His brother, with rather more scientific curiosity, wanted a surgeon to try removing Jeanne's names, an attempt which was abandoned when Jeanne complained: 'Monseigneur, you are hurting me!' Also the Archbishop of Tours arranged for a whole committee of local physicians to examine the hand, their verdict apparently being a favourable one.

Even in the seventeenth century, therefore, there was no lack of critical questioning of stigmatic phenomena, and there is to this day no single obvious explanation for what happened. If Soeur Jeanne's names had been somehow etched into her flesh, Sor Maria's were certainly not. How also should one interpret the early sixteenth century stigmatic Clare de Bugny, whose gushing, apparently sweet-smelling side-wound was examined, with total bafflement, by members of the Padua School of Medicine? Or sixteenth century Francesca de Serrone and seventeenth century Angela della Pace, both of whom had similar side-wounds that were reported to have poured near-scalding blood and water?

All that is certain is that the phenomenon of stigmata can neither be affirmed nor refuted from the evidence, however detailed, of times so much less scientific than our own. With every justification for suspicion, but no absolute proof of overall fraud, we can but now move forward to what can be deduced from the stigmatics who proliferated little more than a century ago, at the start of our own modern age.

4

UNDER SCIENTIFIC
SCRUTINY

ACCORDING to Dr Imbert-Goubeyre's census there were twenty-nine stigmatic cases in his own nineteenth century, a statistic which shows no significant diminution of the phenomenon since its first appearance during the thirteenth century. Indeed Dr Imbert-Goubeyre almost certainly under-estimated, as he appears to have been unaware of two contemporary English stigmatics, Mary Anne Girling, founder of the South London 'People of Sect' (whose apparent manifestation of the stigmata in 1864 caused her to believe herself to be a new incarnation of God) and Liverpool schoolteacher Teresa Higginson, who will be discussed more fully later in this book.

However, well before Mary Anne Girling or Teresa Higginson had come to public attention, much of Europe buzzed with stories of strange stigmatic manifestations associated with yet another nun, Anne Catharine Emmerich from Westphalia in Germany. Unlike St Maria Maddalena de' Pazzi, but in common with many other stigmatics, Anne Catharine had been born into a poor peasant family. As a result of visions since childhood, she longed to be a nun, successfully gaining admission as a postulant, at the age of twenty-eight, in 1802.

According to her own account, she had actually become stigmatised four years earlier, when, like Padre Pio, she had been kneeling deep in prayer before her favourite crucifix. It was an unusual Y-shaped one bearing a particularly skeletal Christ in her parish church of Coesfeld, just a mile and a half from the tiny hamlet of Flamske where she had been born. She had felt in her head 'a strong but not unpleasant glow of warmth'. Then in her own words, strikingly reminiscent of the experiences of St Francis of Assisi and Lukardis of Oberweimar:

> I saw my Divine Spouse under the form of a young man, gloriously aureoled in radiant light, come towards me from the tabernacle of the altar of the Blessed Sacrament. In his left hand he held a garland of fragrant flowers, in his right a crown of thorns. He bade me take from him which I would wear. I stretched out my hand to the crown of thorns. He placed it on my head, and as he withdrew I pressed it firmly on my forehead. At that moment I felt my brows circled with pain ... The next morning my forehead and temples throbbed terribly, and I saw that they were greatly swollen. Several at home remarked on this. The pain and swelling would disappear for a short while, and then return, continuing whole days and nights together. I suffered sadly. A little while after one of my friends said: 'You must put on a clean cap. The one you are wearing is covered with red spots.' After that I took care to arrange my cap and mutch [old German-style close-fitting female head-dress] so as to hide the blood which now began to flow in greater quantities from my head.[1]

Anne Catharine seems to have successfully concealed these early stigmata from her fellow-nuns, but her already impoverished convent community came under severe threat from the repressive rule of Westphalian King Jerome Bonaparte (Napoleon Bonaparte's youngest brother) and was forcibly closed in December 1811. By the spring of 1812 she found some shelter in Dülmen in the form of a hovel-like room in the house of a widow, Frau Roters. But by the November she was bed-ridden, and on 29 December, the anniversary of the martyrdom of St Thomas of Canterbury, she received the full stigmata while a vision of Jesus appeared to her with wounds that 'shone like so many furnaces of light', and felt as if they burnt into her flesh. In the wake of this incident Frau Roters' daughter found her bleeding so heavily from hands, feet and side that she thought she had suffered an accident, and called her mother.

Although Anne Catharine begged the Roters to remain silent and they kindly bandaged the wounds, the news inevitably leaked out. On 23 March the following year she was visited by the sceptical young local physician, Dr Frantz Wilhelm Westener. After giving her a thorough examination, Westener pronounced himself convinced of the genuineness of her stigmata, a verdict which inevitably provoked further investigation, this time under the auspices of the local ecclesiastical authorities. Between 13 and 23 June 1813 a team of twenty doctors observed Catharine in round-the-clock relays. They confirmed, in a report signed on 23 June, that throughout their observation period there had been no physical interference with her wounds.

From this point Anne Catharine, popularly dubbed 'the Living Crucifix', became something of a celebrity and within a matter of weeks was provided with an improved, though still tiny, lodging. Her stigmata continued to bleed and to pain her constantly until the end of 1819. Then they reappeared intermittently on certain appropriate days and she continued to be bedridden right up to her death in 1824. The constant stream of visitors, although distressing to her at the time, at least had the benefit for posterity that she was well-observed. In particular the poet Clemens Brentano, a friend of Goethe, spent much of the last five and a half years of her life at her bedside recording for subsequent publication[2] what she told him of her visions of Jesus's earthly life and death, and the later histories of some of his disciples, and of his mother Mary.

And this improved observation of stigmatics, along with a proliferation of the phenomenon among laywomen as well as nuns, became typical of the rationalist nineteenth century. Such scrutiny was a feature of the case of a young Tyrolean girl, Domenica Lazzari, stigmatised no more than ten years after Anne Catharine Emmerich's death, and who attracted attention from some well-educated and questioning young Englishmen.

Of origins equally as humble as Anne Catharine's, Domenica Lazzari was born on 16 March 1815 in the village of Capriana in the Italian Tyrol, reachable in the early nineteenth century only by a strenuous four hour hike from the nearest main village of Cavalese. When Domenica was only thirteen her miller father died, an eventuality which reduced her to paroxysms of the most intense grief. Five years later, following an unspecified incident during which she spent a terrifying night alone in a mill, she suffered a paralysis which caused her, like Anne Catharine, to remain bedridden for the rest of her life.

Also as in the case of Anne Catharine, Domenica's stigmata were swift to follow. On 10 January 1834 wounds suddenly opened up in both her hands, both feet and her left side. These began to regularly reopen each Friday, just as had those of Lukardis of Oberweimar more than five centuries before. After another three weeks her forehead broke out in puncture marks as from a crown of thorns, which she explained to her family with the words 'During the night a very beautiful lady came to my bedside and set a crown upon my head.'[3]

From 10 April – and again there is a parallel with Anne Catharine Emmerich and several previous stigmatics – Domenica purportedly gave up eating anything apart from a communion water once or twice a week. Also, as has been noted of St Francis in his last years, she developed an exaggerated aversion to strong stimuli: bright sunlight, vibrant sounds, sugar placed on her tongue, even the gentlest pressure on her abdomen. And in a manner we have seen repeatedly among female stigmatics, she went into terrifying convulsions. As described by one physician who studied her closely, Dr Leonardo Dei Cloche:

> Domenica with her tightly clasped hands often showered blows upon her breast with intense violence, so that the noise was past belief.[4]

Reminiscent of Lukardis of Oberweimar, whose breast-beatings were heard all over the convent, Domenica's thumpings sometimes fell at the rate of more than 400 an hour, and were heard more than sixty feet from her house. Yet despite such exertions and lack of food, every Friday her wounds continued to discharge one to two ounces of blood, lessening only with the course of years.

Domenica's native Capriana was a remote hamlet even by the standards of the nineteenth century. Nonetheless, news of her eventually spread to England, where three Oxford-educated young men, Thomas William Allies, the rector of Launton, Oxfordshire, and his friends J.H. Pollen and J.H. Wynne, all decided to make a special visit to her as part of their Grand Tour of France and Italy during the summer of 1847. Regrettably, by the time they made this visit, Domenica, although still only thirty-two, was already well past the most vigorous stage of her manifestations, and so depleted in energy that she was a mere nine months from death. Even so, the Englishmen's observations are particularly valuable for their cautious, objective and scientific approach.

Knowing that Domenica produced her bleedings on a Friday, they timed their arrival for a Thursday – so that they might observe her before and during these occurrences. Wynne described the scene that confronted them when they entered Domenica's home on the Thursday:

> At the inner end of a low room near the wall, in a bed hardly larger than a crib, Domenica lay crouched up, the hands closely clasped over the breast, the head a little raised, the legs gathered up nearly under her, in a way the bed clothes did not allow us to see. About three quarters of an inch under the roots of the hair a straight line is draw[n] all round the forehead, dotted with small punctures a quarter of an inch apart; above this the flesh is of the natural colour, perfectly clear and free from blood; below the face is covered down to the bottom of the nose, and the cheeks to the same extent, with a dry crust or mask of blood. Her breast heaved with a sort of convulsion, and her teeth chattered.
>
> On the outside of both hands, as they lie clasped together, in a line with the second finger about an inch from the knuckle, is a hard scar, of a dark colour, rising above the flesh, half an inch in length, by about three eighths of an inch in width; round these the skin slightly reddened, but quite free from blood. From the position of the hands it is not possible to see well inside, but stooping down on the right of her bed I could almost see an incision answering to the outward one, and apparently deeper . . . She looked at us very fixedly, but hardly spoke. We heard her only cry 'Dio mio' several times when her pains were bad . . . . By far the most striking point in her appearance this evening was that dry mask of blood descending so regularly from the puncture line round the forehead; for it must be remarked that the blood has flowed in a straight line all down the face, as if she were erect, not as it would naturally flow from the position in which she was lying, that is, off the middle to the sides of the face.[5]

Faithful to their plan, the English trio ensured that they were punctually at Domenica's bedside by five thirty the next morning, all noting with astonishment the 'very remarkable' change that had come over her wounds. As again reported by Wynne:

> The hard scars on the outside of her hands had sunk to the level of the flesh, and become raw and fresh running wounds, but without indentation, from which there was a streak of blood running a finger's length, not perpendicularly, but down the middle of the wrist. The wound inside the left hand seemed

on the contrary deep and furrowed, much blood had flowed, and the hand seemed mangled; the wound of the right hand inside could not be seen. The punctures round the forehead had been bleeding, and were open, so that the mask of blood was thicker, and very terrible to look at. The darkest place of all was the tip of the nose ... The sight is so fearful that a person of weak nerves would very probably be overcome by it.[6]

Given that so far we have still not eliminated the possibility that the stigmatics' wounds were self-inflicted, could the impoverished Domenica's bleedings have been merely a trick to wring money from credulous visitors? Certainly this was not the impression gained by Allies and his companions. As commented by Wynne:

Nothing can be more simple and natural than her [Domenica's] manner and that of her sister. Their cottage is open at all times. Domenica may be closely seen, all but touched and handled ...

Pollen remarked that they had talked to Domenica's sister. They found that she:

was perfectly simple, wanted no money, and treated her sister more as an invalid than anything else.

And as Wynne concluded with the rest:

No eye witness, I will venture to say, will ever receive the notion of anything like deceit.

Yet although they were conscientious observers, and their remarks were independently corroborated by Italian physician Dr Dei Cloche, Allies, Pollen and Wynne (all of whom went on to become converts to Roman Catholicism) were not medical specialists. But three years after Domenica's death, in a one-storey cottage in Bois d'Haine, Belgium, there was born yet again of poor peasant stock another stigmatic, Louise Lateau, who would receive the most intensive medical investigation of any stigmatic so far.

In Louise Lateau we yet again come across a stigmatic who had suffered a serious early-life mishap. At thirteen years old Louise was knocked down and trampled by a cow, receiving apparently serious internal injuries which initially she tried to ignore, despite severe pain from abscesses. Four years later she was beset by throat trouble of sufficient seriousness that she was given the Last Sacrament, shortly followed by blood-spitting and more abscesses. A year later, in 1868, she reached a point near death where she seemed to receive visions and talked to heavenly visitors.

But she recovered, and at the beginning of 1869 began to manifest the first signs of the stigmata. On the first Friday in January she felt intense pain in her hands, feet and side, even though no marks were yet perceptible. On 24 April the first blood began oozing from her left side, followed a week later by the first bleeding from the upper surface of her feet, then a few weeks later the commencement of bleeding from her hands. From 17 July she was a full stigmatic, having ecstatic experiences and bleedings which she manifested with clockwork regularity every Friday up to her death at the age of thirty-three, an estimated total of some 800 separate occurrences.

It was this regularity which led to her being subjected to the closest scientific scrutiny. In line with the rapid advances in medicine at this time, all the surviving documentation on Louise is more exact than anything which had gone before.

From reports by her doctors Lefebvre, Bourneville and others, we know that her stigmata went through a complete weekly cycle. This would begin each Tuesday with a burning sensation in the areas of her wounds, reminiscent of the itching reported by Jane Hunt, which continued during the Wednesday and Thursday. By the Thursday evening headaches added to Louise's discomfort, accompanied by a hot and dry skin, and rapid irregular pulse. All these symptoms steadily increased in intensity until the appearance of blisters marking the onset of stigmata proper. According to Dr Lefebvre:

> On each of the reddish surfaces of the hands and feet a blister is seen to appear and gradually rise; when it is fully developed it forms a rounded, hemispheric protrusion on the surface of the skin; its base is of the same dimensions as the reddish surface on which it rests, that is, about two and a half centimetres long and one and a half wide. . . . This blister is full of limpid serum. However, it often takes the colour of a more or less dark red on the palms of the hands and the soles of the feet. . . . The zone of skin surrounding the blister is not the seat of any turgescence or reddening.[7]

Louise's bleedings would usually take place during the early hours of Friday, often beginning with her side, where the wound would be between the fifth and sixth ribs, a little below the middle of her left breast. In this particular location and the crown of thorns wounds around her forehead the blood issued from almost imperceptible points in the skin even while Dr Lefebvre and other investigators, who included Dr Imbert Goubeyre, watched with the aid of a magnifying glass. The 'nail' wound blisters would independently rise from light pinkish areas permanently in the centre of Louise's hands, both on the back and in the palms, the blood subsequently welling up through crevasse-like openings in the flesh. She would also manifest on her right shoulder an area of four square centimetres of apparent abrasion, as from the carrying of something like a heavy cross.

So perplexing was all this to Dr Lefebvre and his colleagues that they racked their brains for ways to guard against any possibility of Louise deceiving them. These procedures were vigorously objected to by Louise's father on the grounds that they were an insult to his daughter's honesty:

> They think my daughters liars, do they? They think it is we who have made Louise bleed! Did I ever ask anyone to come and see her? All I ask is they should leave us alone![8]

Fortunately Louise was more amenable than her parents. Even as early as the age of eighteen, the first year in which she had been stigmatised, she unstintingly made herself available to Lefebvre and his colleagues for the most rigorous tests they could devise. Quaint though they may sound to us today, the elaborateness and seriousness of these is evident from Dr Lefebvre's descriptions:

> On Wednesday 26 December 1868, in the morning, after the surfaces of the hands and feet had been seen to be quite intact, a leather glove was applied to each hand, tightly drawn, fixed and sealed round the wrist. These gloves were cut like mittens so as not to impede her work, and to avoid the notice of her mother. A shoe was fixed in a similar manner to one of her feet.
> On the next day, Thursday, Dr Lecrinier, M. Dupont of Fayt and M. Didry, the schoolmaster of Bois d'Haine, satisfied themselves that these objects and their seals were completely intact and that it was impossible to touch the stigmatic surfaces of the hands and the foot without displacing them. These

gentlemen thought it advisable to remove the glove from one of the hands, so they broke the fastening of the glove on the left hand and took it off. There was neither blister nor redness. The glove which had been taken off was then replaced and sealed up again.

On Friday morning, after confirming that the three objects were completely intact, Dr Spiltoir de Marchienne, in the presence of eight witnesses, took off the two gloves and the shoe. This was what was observed: the blood was flowing freely from the stigmata in the palms of both hands and overflowed the gloves everywhere. On the stigmata on the backs of both hands, which were not yet bleeding, the blisters were completely developed. The two feet were in the same state; on the left, which had been sealed up, as on the right, which had not been made the object of any precautions, the blisters were completely developed. The bleeding only began later.[9]

But could Louise still have somehow inflicted the wounds on herself, perhaps by striking herself on something that caused the injuries through the gloves? To overcome even this objection on Thursday 21 January 1875 a Dr Warlomont devised the new test of substituting for the flexible glove a solid glass cylinder encasing Louise's whole arm. He described this:

It is a crystal globe fourteen centimetres in diameter. It is provided, at one of the poles of extremities of the cylinder, with a neck similar to that of an ordinary bottle; at the other end there is another neck of nine centimetres diameter. The former is closed by a cork stopper, pierced by a bent tube of crystal, which on the inside does not extend beyond the end of the neck. The inner end of this neck, like that of the tube, is covered with a metal mesh, which does not prevent the access of air, but does prevent the introduction of any wounding instrument; a precaution which is unnecessary, in view of the tube being bent at an acute angle, making it practically impossible to introduce any kind of rod inside the receptacle.

Neck and tube are joined by several wax seals, the second neck is fitted with a sleeve of rubber sheeting, attached to its outer edge with a glue of rubber dissolved in naphtha, which gives it strong adhesion and makes it impossible to detach without much tearing. But for greater security this part of the

glove is covered with a narrow bracelet of rubber , fixed to
the globe on one side, to the said bracelet [sic] and to the edge
of the sleeve on the other. This fixing is accomplished by five
wax seals.

I chose the right arm precisely because of the scapular stigma
[Louise's apparent 'carrying of the cross' wound on her
shoulder] which is on the right. As we were going to condemn
the whole limb to immobility for twenty hours, we thought
it wiser to choose the right arm, which would soon be reduced
to helplessness by the pains in that shoulder. As these pains
did in fact accompany the scapular stigma, we preferred to
leave Louise the use of her left arm. [10]

At 10.30 on the Friday morning, with Louise in pain from the
stigmata and the shoulder wound, Dr Warlomont and Dr Crocq
began removing the seals. Dr Crocq noted:

The right hand was enclosed in the apparatus applied by
M. Warlomont the previous day. This was perfectly intact; so
were the reinforcements of rubber sheeting and gutta percha
[an early form of latex]. The lower end of the receptacle was
occupied by a little pool of diffluent liquid blood, not more than
five grammes in quantity. The back of the hand, which we saw
first, showed clots of coagulated blood, black, hard and
adhering strongly, covering at that time the surface of the
dorsal stigmatic wound and preventing the flow of blood,
which explains the relatively small quantity of liquid blood
found in the apparatus. Having removed the latter, we
detached these clots, more than one of which stuck firmly to
the base of the wound; and this was followed by the
reappearance of a haemorrhage, persistent but not abundant.
The wound which produced it was about a centimetre and a
half long and five millimetres wide. Its epidermis had
disappeared; the base occupied by the dermis was red and,
as it were, muddy; some small black clots could be seen in
it. The whole rested on a perfectly mobile hardening of the
dermis.

Warlomont concluded from the experiments:

It seems to me, therefore, that the haemorrhages really
appeared spontaneously and without the intervention of
external violence.

39

Effectively then, these scientific tests on Louise Lateau went as far as any up to the present time. They indicate that in the case of Louise at least, something genuinely spontaneous and free from physical contrivance was responsible for her bleedings.

That there was something even to the bizarre names sported by Soeur Jeanne des Anges two centuries previously seemed evident from similar studies of a Breton peasant girl, Marie-Julie Jahenny. Born around 1853 in the unfortunately-named hamlet of La Fraudais near Nantes, Marie-Julie Jahenny was first stigmatised when she was twenty. As in so many cases, she received wounds to her hands, feet and side, all of which appeared on 21 March 1873. Then a 'crown of thorns', apparently with punctures as large as hemp seeds, manifested on 5 October, followed six weeks later by an imprint on her left shoulder, as from the carrying of a cross. Two weeks after that nail wounds appeared on the outer sides of her hands and feet, to match those that had previously appeared on the inner. On 12 January 1874 she added to her decorations cord-like marks on her wrists, as where Jesus would have been bound. On the same day a form of emblematic pattern appeared over her heart, followed two days later by scourge-like weals on her ankles, legs and forearms.

Dr Imbert-Goubeyre, while taking the closest interest in the experiments on Louise Lateau, also came to hear of this new and equally astonishing case. He journeyed to La Fraudais to observe Marie-Julie's further manifestations, some of which, like Soeur Jeanne, she predicted so that they could be observed as they happened. Dr Imbert-Goubeyre reported in 1875:

> She announced a month beforehand that she was shortly to receive a new stigmatisation, and that a cross and flower with the words 'O crux ave' were to be impressed upon her breast. More than a week before the event occurred she named the precise day: it was to be 7 December. The day before this her breast was examined, when it was ascertained that the emblems spoken of had not yet made their appearance. On the morrow, before the ecstasy came on, she offered to submit to another examination, but this was considered unnecessary; she had the right to expect that we should take her word for it. Soon after she passed into a state of trance, and ... when the ecstasy was over, the cross, the flower and the inscription could be clearly seen upon her breast.[11]

It sounds strikingly like the names reported on the hand of

Soeur Jeanne des Anges. They appear to have been of similar permanence, for nearly twenty years later, in his book of 1894, Dr Imbert Goubeyre asserted, apparently from a recent examination of Marie-Julie, that 'the flower and the inscription are visible still.'

Though we may be impressed that a distinguished professor of medicine found such stigmatics so convincing, a word of caution is needed. Domenica Lazzari was clearly devout, but there was nothing particularly saintly about her. Even allowing for Gallic lesser reserve over such matters, there is something a little disquieting about Marie-Julie having been so liberal with displays of her breast for elderly gentlemen like Dr Imbert, not to mention the other witnesses she and her family drew together for each astonishing performance.

This need for caution is reinforced when we learn that among the four stigmatics whom Dr Imbert knew and examined personally, two of whom were Louise and Marie-Julie, a third, though equally warmly remarked on by him, gave rise to the most serious independent questioning of her integrity. This was Palma Matarelli, yet another peasant woman, quite illiterate, from Oria near Brindisi in southern Italy. She manifested stigmata in May 1857, four years after having been widowed at the age of twenty-eight. Palma would produce miraculous Communion hosts on her tongue, sometimes of a variety purportedly teleported from St Peter's in Rome. Although her stigmata consisted only of the wound in the side and 'crown of thorns' by the time Dr Imbert journeyed to Oria in 1871, he wrote of her enthusiastically in the 1873 edition of his book *Les Stigmatisées*:

> I have witnessed the most extraordinary manifestations during
> the few days I spent in her vicinity . . . I have twice seen her
> on fire inside her clothes, ascertaining afterwards that there
> were real burns in her flesh similar to those caused by a boiling
> liquid. I have also seen the linen cloths laid upon her heart
> during this conflagration marked with extraordinary patterns
> when they were removed. I have further seen the blood trickle
> from the circlet of punctures upon her forehead, and as it was
> caught in the handkerchief I held under it I watched it trace
> out patterns like those of the 'conflagration'.[12]

But within two years of these words being published, the French Monsignor Barbier de Montault was told, in a private audience, by Pope Pius IX:

> I have had an investigation made concerning Palma. In consequence of the report which was then drawn up ... take good heed ... of what I tell you. What Palma is doing is the work of the devil, and her pretended miraculous Communions with hosts taken from St Peter's are a pure piece of trickery. It is all imposture, and I have the proofs here in the drawer of my bureau. She has befooled a whole crowd of pious and credulous souls. One of your fellow-countrymen has written a book about her which has been delated to the Holy Office. Out of consideration for the author, who is a good Catholic, and whose intentions are excellent, the Holy Office decided not to condemn him publicly, but has begged him to withdraw the book from circulation.[13]

Exactly what those proofs were has never been disclosed, although presumably they lie to this day within the Vatican's secret archives. But there can be no doubt that the 'fellow-countryman' of Barbier de Montault was Dr Imbert-Goubeyre, and the book the second volume of his *Les Stigmatisées* which specifically describes his researches on Palma Matarelli. This was never reprinted, and his references to her were much curtailed in his book of 1894.

The effect of this might be like a cold bath on all the other scientific researches on stigmatics during the nineteenth century, particularly since Vatican secrecy precludes us from knowing the exact details of Palma's imposture. It is easy to anticipate that some of Palma's methods, particularly those in respect of the miraculous hosts, were probably mere conjuring tricks. But what of the manifestation of blood, apparently witnessed before Dr Imbert's own eyes? Still bewildered, we can but conclude our skip through the stigmatics of history, and now look at those living closest to, if not actually in, our own time.

$\smile$ 5 $\smile$

INTO THE TWENTIETH CENTURY

WITH the new knowledge of the twentieth century it might be thought easier to determine the validity of stigmata once and for all. There is still little sign of any diminution of the phenomenon, for even my own comparatively modest researches suggest around ten stigmatics living at the present time. Photography has been developed to a fine art, including latterly the facility for television and video cameras to document and supplement verbal descriptions of stigmatic wounds. Theoretically, with all our scientific advances, we should have far more sophisticated means of ascertaining what is happening than the Heath Robinson contrivances used on Louise Lateau by Dr Lefebvre and his colleagues. In practice the situation is not so simple, readily demonstrated by one of the twentieth century's first cases, contemporary with the earliest years of Padre Pio's stigmata, that of Bertha Mrazek, or as she preferred to style herself, Georges Marasco.

Bertha was around thirty years of age when in the summer of 1920 she sprang to public attention in a most dramatic way on visiting the shrine of Notre Dame at Halle, some ten miles south east of Brussels. This shrine had long been famed for a statue claimed to have something of the same healing powers as Lourdes. But there had been few claims in modern times until a dramatic report published on 27 July in Belgium's *Libre Belgique*:

A correspondent writes from the little town of Halle that the population . . . is greatly excited over an extraordinary event. On Monday 19 July, about three in the afternoon, a motor-car drove up with four visitors – a sick girl, thirty years of age, who lives at Forest [a Brussels suburb]; the Very Rev Curé of Forest; a nurse; and a young soldier, M.J—, who had fought in the war. A stretcher was procured from the hospital and the sick girl was carried in and taken to the shrine. Clothed in a long nightdress, she was set down at the foot of the altar, deadly pale and without sign of life. During the journey she had fainted and M.le Curé had been afraid that they would never get her out of the motor alive.

Before the miraculous statue they spent a quarter of an hour in trying to revive her. At last recovering her senses, she asked for M.le Curé, who came to her and said: 'I am here, your parish priest; we are at the shrine of Halle before Our Lady's statue. Have confidence and pray.'

Suddenly the sick girl who had been paralysed for a year and blind for two months, lifted her arms, joined her hands and staggered forward for a step or two. They caught her and laid her down again. But she rose a second time, climbed up the steps of the altar unaided, and there knelt down and prayed fervently. She said to M.le Curé, 'I am entirely cured. Look at my hands – and besides, I can see.'[1]

That 'cured' girl was Bertha Mrazek, apparently the daughter of a Belgian mother and Czechoslovak father. She seems to have been a most colourful person, having before her illnesses apparently worked with the legendary Nurse Edith Cavell, and been twice sentenced to death by the Germans during the First World War. According to all available information she really had been confined to bed throughout the previous year. So serious had been her physical condition that her feet and her hands had been completely paralysed, some of her bones had been dislocated, seven vertebrae were out of place, her jaw had been twisted, and she had been blind for the previous two months. Her doctor and neighbours were said to have been astonished to learn of the transformation at the Halle shrine.

To compound this sensation, within three years of her cure, at Easter 1923, Bertha manifested her purported new miracle – stigmatisation. As apparent proof of this one of her admirers sent to the Rev Herbert Thurston, England's foremost authority on stigmatics, a set of photographs.[2] Two of these showed Bertha, now with mannish hair-styling and emphatically calling herself Georges Marasco, sitting up in bed and displaying the wounds in her hands and side. A third, a close-up of her legs, revealed bruises as if from falls carrying the cross, and with what appeared to be nail wounds in the feet. Thurston's informant told him in her accompanying letter:

> I am not an expert in photography, and so have not obtained a very good result, especially in the photo which shows the stigmata in the hands. They showed much more in reality than appears in the print . . . as you see from the other photo the stigmata hardly show on the backs of the hands. Inside they are very distinctly marked, and a curious thing is that they show much more against the light, than with the light full upon them as it is in the photo.[3]

Thurston's correspondent also added that seven punctures in the forehead from a purported crown of thorns were easily visible to anyone studying 'Georges' in daylight, and there were also others at the back of the head concealed by her hair. She went on:

> The wounds in the feet show clearly and you will also see the dreadful bruises on the legs. They came suddenly and were almost red at first, and vanished only after Easter Day. The side, as you perceive, is very visible. I have seen it several times in different aspects. It was bleeding on Good Friday, but only just for a little while, during the acute time of her crucifixion. I saw it immediately afterwards and also the quite fresh stains of blood on her linen. I had seen it several times before Good Friday (it had been opened on Friday, the 16th, at Holy Mass during the consecration) and I saw it on the 19th, covered with a scab which seemed to be formed of a sort of serum rather than deep red blood. Then it healed gradually until it was only a very red mark. Afterwards it opened once more in Holy Week and bled, as I told you, on Good Friday. Many people whom I know (about ten or more) have seen the wound in different stages. To have to show the wound in the side is one of the trials which Georges finds very painful. You may notice this in the expression of her face.[4]

Thurston subsequently commented in an article he wrote for the Roman Catholic journal *The Month* a little more than a year after receiving this correspondence:

> I am bound to say that from my own acquaintance with the

person who took these photographs, from the verbal
description which accompanied them, and from the
circumstances under which they were obtained, I am satisfied
that the wounds are real and that they cannot have been self-
inflicted.[5]

According to Thurston, in common with several other stigmatics, including Jane Hunt, 'Georges' claimed to take on and suffer
the illnesses of others, often needing to remain in bed because
of the pain of these afflictions. Like Jane, she also appeared to
converse with holy beings, including angels and saints. From the
messages these brought, she claimed to have been chosen for
a mysterious mission of world-shattering significance.

Yet as Thurston, ever the scrupulous and fairminded scholar,
also felt bound to reveal, he had just learned of some astonishing
developments in Belgium which shed a less favourable light on
Bertha. As a result of some undisclosed misdemeanours, Bertha
had been arrested. Newspaper investigations had found her to
have lied in various respects, and to have obtained money under
false pretences. It emerged that after leaving home at an early
age she had joined a circus, where she had tried everything from
lion-taming and bareback riding to working as female contortion-
ist. The little girl who lived with Bertha, and whom Bertha always
introduced as her sister, was shown to be her daughter from a
pre-war adulterous affair with an artist. Most damning of all,
because of the seriousness of Bertha's various deceptions, by
which she had extorted large sums of money, a psychiatric report
on her had been called for, which concluded, as summarised in
La Nation Belge:

From her childhood the accused has presented physical and
mental symptoms of hysteria. She frequently falls into
secondary states which make themselves perceptible by a
disintegration (*dédoublement*) of personality and by mystical
tendencies pathological in origin. Over people of weak mind
she exercises an unhealthy influence, because they are
contagiously affected by her own mental state. In our opinion,
therefore, the accused is suffering from a hysterical psychosis
complicated by mystical ravings and manifestations of
mythomania (mania for romancing). She was in a condition of
dementia at the time when the incidents occurred for which
she is being prosecuted. In the interests both of mental health

and public safety it is necessary that the Court should dispose of her future.[6]

Adjudged insane as a result of this report, Bertha was duly transferred from prison to a mental asylum at Mons, after which her ultimate fate appears to have gone unrecorded.

There can be little doubt that the Belgian authorities had good grounds for making the judgment they did. But as in the case of the Vatican's denunciation of Palma Matarelli, such a verdict on Bertha Mrazek is unsatisfactory for the questions it does not answer. It clearly tends to confirm a pattern from our earlier examples, namely that stigmata are frequently associated with hysteria and neurosis as much as saintliness. Moreover, now that we know that Bertha received circus training, it is plausible to suggest that she may have learned some sleight-of-hand tricks which helped her fake her stigmata. But we still have no hard evidence that she actually did fake her stigmata.

The grounds for serious misgivings about the genuineness of stigmatic wounds increase when we turn to another twentieth century stigmatic, arguably the best known and best documented of this century next to Padre Pio, Germany's Therese Neumann[7], who came to public attention within months of the asylum door closing on Bertha Mrazek.

A native of the rustic Bavarian village of Konnersruth, close to the border with Czechoslovakia, Therese was born in 1898. She was the eldest daughter of a devoutly Catholic tailor and his wife, who subsequently provided her with no less than nine surviving brothers and sisters. Reportedly an intelligent if hyperactive child, when she was fourteen Therese went out to work at a local inn which had farmland attached, and here because of her vigour she was quickly chosen for duties in the fields.

She seems to have been enjoying a happy enough life – despite two apparent rape attempts – when tragedy suddenly struck. On 10 March 1918 fire broke out in a house next to the inn where Therese worked, and when the inn itself became threatened Therese was soon in the thick of the action, heaving pails of water up to the innkeeper as he fought to save his roof. After two hours of this work something suddenly seemed to snap in the small of her back, and she was forced to return home bent double from the pain. Although after a few days in bed she was back on her feet, she was no longer as fit as she had been, complaining of difficulties eating, and falling in a faint while fetching potatoes from a cellar.

Her health continued to deteriorate, notably in the form of head-aches and embarrassing soiling of her bed. This she blamed on the younger sister with whom she shared the bed. Hospitalised, and discharging herself against medical advice, she began suffer-ing convulsions, leading in March 1919 to one in which she lost her sight, even though a medical examination showed that her pupils reacted normally to light. More problems followed. Leaning out of bed to feed her pet pigeon, she suffered paralysis of her left side, and became unable to hear with her left ear or to speak. During the summer of 1919, while being helped out of bed by her parents, she fell unconscious, subsequently going rigid and becoming paralysed in both legs. She stayed in this condition for the next four years, with added gastric complications during the latter period. She seemed as abject an invalid as Bertha Mrazek had been before being taken to Halle.

Then came 29 April, 1923, just four days after Pope Pius IX in Rome had solemnly beatified her namesake, Thérèse of Lisieux. The Lisieux Thérèse had died, aged only twenty four, the year before Therese Neumann had been born. At six in the morning Therese's father looked in on her before setting off for the next village to buy her some herb tea. There seemed to be no change. But half an hour later, after saying a prayer to Thérèse of Lisieux, and dreaming that someone was touching her pillow, Therese woke up, opened her eyes, and announced that she could see, remarking on how much her brothers and sisters had grown dur-ing the time she had been blind.

Konnersreuth was a tiny, close-knit community, and inevitably news of the 'cure' caused a local sensation. Nonetheless, Therese remained paralysed, prey to more stomach problems and further convulsions, one of which caused her left leg to become so drawn up against her right thigh that she was obliged to remain perma-nently on her back. The bedsores became so acute that there was even concern that her left foot might need to be amputated.

Then came 17 May, 1925, the day that in Rome Thérèse of Lisieux was being canonised as 'Saint Teresa of the Child Jesus and the Holy Face'. That afternoon Therese's parents heard her cry out and on entering her room found her in a seeming trance, talking with some presence whom they could not see. Suddenly, without any help on their part, she sat up and stretched her hands forward, towards where a picture of Thérèse of Lisieux hung on the wall. She then fell back, and when her mother attended to the bedclothes she saw that Therese's left leg, previously so awkwardly twisted, had straightened up and was now lying perfectly naturally alongside her right.

While seeming still partly in trance, Therese called for the parish priest, Father Naber. When he arrived she announced that she would now be able to sit up, and even walk. A dress was brought for her, and to everyone's astonishment she got out of bed and took a few steps. She subsequently explained that she had seen a beautiful light from which had come a voice asking if she wished to be cured. Although she had replied that she wanted only whatever was God's will, the voice told her that while she would have much more to suffer, the ability to walk would now be restored to her.

During the subsequent days strength gradually returned to her legs and within a month, for the first time in years, she was able to walk to church with the aid of a stick, much to the marvel of the local populace. On 30 September, the anniversary of Thérèse of Lisieux's death, the light and the voice returned once more to tell her that she would be able to walk totally unaided. Again this proved to be the case.

Six weeks later, on 13 November, Therese's temperature rose alarmingly, and she complained of severe pains. Diagnosing acute appendicitis, her physician, Dr Seidl, was in the midst of arranging her admission to hospital, when she reported another experience of the light and the voice, and professed to have received yet another cure. Whatever the explanation, the appendicitis never returned.

But for us the most significant of Therese's 'miraculous' happenings took place the next year, during the run-up to Easter. Still suffering from headaches and abscesses in her ears, during the night of Thursday 4 May to Friday 5 May she reportedly lay musing on Jesus's passion, when, in her own words, as recorded by contemporary biographer Friedrich Von Lama:

> All at once I saw the Redeemer before me. I saw him in the
> Garden of the Mount of Olives. When this happened to me
> the first time, I did not know it had a special meaning. But
> I saw the Saviour as he knelt there . . . Suddenly I felt, while
> I saw the Saviour, such a pain in my side that I thought: 'Now
> I am going to die.' At the same time I felt something hot run
> down my side. It was blood. It kept trickling until towards
> noon of the next day.[8]

Although a wound had apparently opened up in her side, Therese said nothing to her parents. She also swore to silence her sister Zenzl, with whom she shared her room and who had noticed her trying to hide a cloth soaked in blood. The next two Fridays Therese again experienced the Mount of Olives vision, with the addition in the first week of scenes from Jesus's scourging and crowning with thorns, and in the second of his carrying the cross to Calvary. Again she apparently bled from the wound in the side, and another wound also broke out on the back of her left hand. But still she kept everything a secret.

Then there came the night of Maundy Thursday to Good Friday, 1926. From 10 pm on the Thursday through to 3 pm the following day Therese reportedly 'saw' Jesus's entire Passion, up to and including the Crucifixion. Accompanying these visions her side-wound reportedly bled yet more profusely, and there appeared for the first time full nail-wounds in her hands and feet. It was now impossible to keep all this from her parents, and they, astonished, sent for Father Naber and for Dr Seidl, neither of whom could offer any rational explanation. All attempts by Dr Seidl to use ointments to help the wounds heal seemed only to cause swelling and increased pain, and it was accordingly adjudged better to leave them alone. Soon all the village knew of the fresh sensation, and the news began to circulate throughout Germany and overseas. Tiny, insignificant Konnersreuth had its own full-blown stigmatic.

Like those of Domenica Lazzari and others, Therese's wounds fell into a pattern of manifesting on most Fridays, and persisted throughout the remaining thirty-six years of her life. It might be thought that they would be among the best observed of those of any stigmatic. In practice, however, wherever she went outside she covered herself as modestly as any nun. She disliked being photographed except by people she knew. And although there have survived an adequate number of photographs that show her wounds, these are chiefly in black and white.

Among these, some are dramatic close-ups of her propped up in bed with blood pouring from beneath her eyelids. One, taken in her bedroom on Easter morning 1936, shows her left palm with a modest indentation as from a nail. There are also several which show the nail-wounds in the backs of her hands. These significantly changed in shape over the years, from round to distinctively square.

But even these are not above suspicion, particularly since the only certain photographer to whom I have found reference has been Ferdinand Neumann, Therese's brother. So how sure can we be that her wounds were not contrived in some way, perhaps even with the help of her family? In particular, even though we know Father Naber and others fervently believed in her, did anyone outside the Neumann family independently and reliably observe any of her bleeding actually commence?

As early as 1928 there was concern to establish the answers to such questions. A special Thursday to Friday overnight observation of Therese, instigated by the local bishopric, was held at her home on 22/23 March, with Father Naber in attendance and the none too enthusiastic co-operation of the Neumann family. Those acting as observers included Monsignor Buchberger, Bishop of Ratisbon, Mgr. Hierl, the Suffragan Bishop, and Professors Killermann, Hilgreiner and Stöckl, all under the supervision of Professor Martini, director of the University Hospital of Bonn. Professor Martini's subsequent report, with careful, timed notes of all that was observed, makes most interesting reading. The following are the most significant extracts:

0.45 am ... Therese sits up quickly. During this time, while complaining that she is too hot, Therese has lifted her cover two or three times so that one can see no more than her head. Behind the cover she makes movements with her arms and draws her leg up so that her knee appears on the left side of the bed and her left foot hangs out.

1.05 am. The wound of the left hand is covered with a little blood ...

1.25 am. Killerman rises at the moment when she draws up her cover and tells me that now the wound of the heart is bleeding. I look at it but believe that it is only a little blood put there from the wounds of the hands. At the moment when we turn round, both parents cry out: 'This is against modesty.' They themselves go usually out and did remain only today ...

2.58 am. Stöckl comes.

3.05 am. We both must leave the room, she thinks. (That means she wants to relieve herself.) From the outside we hear her sigh very much.

3.10 am. The wound on the left hand seems much more full of blood. The face, too, is stained with fresh, moist blood.

3.30 am. The blood on the left hand has become dry.[9]

Martini then recorded that there was no more significant activity throughout the rest of the night, and that when Bishop Buch-berger, apparently at the Neumann family's insistence, left Ther-ese alone at about 8.15 am, the headcloth with which she seems to have constantly covered her hair was quite definitely still clean. Yet a mere ten minutes later, on Suffragan Bishop Hierl's re-entry, it was immediately spotted that 'this same headcloth was already completely soaked with blood.' Martini goes on:

> 8.35 am. Much blood on the left hand. The face is completely covered with it. The headcloth is soaked . . .
>
> c. 11.30 am. The father or the parents complain that the air is bad. I go out with the Bishop, but before that I observe that there is only dry blood on the left hand and also about the eyes. I ask Killerman and Hilgreiner to make sure of this, and they notice it too. I ask them to observe when and how the bleeding begins again. The Bishop, on leaving, recommends that always at least one of the gentlemen should stay in the room.
>
> *Remark:* At noon Killerman and Hilgreiner tell me that there was nothing to be done, that they both had to leave the room owing to the insistence of the mother. She told them that about this time Therese always needed at least one hour's complete rest, and that today, too, she must rest for some time quite alone. When they returned, all was red with fresh blood.[10]

From all this Martini felt bound to conclude:

> I have never seen one of Therese Neumann's wounds actually bleeding. At the moment I came in, at 11.45 pm, her eyes were so full of blood that it was impossible to observe the conjunctivae or the other parts of the eyes which could have bled: the blood was flowing down both cheeks. So I tried to observe the beginning of the bleeding of the hands, especially of the left hand, which was more accessible to observation. This observation was a priori made more difficult by the permanent presence of the stigmata. This alteration of the normal state made it more difficult to observe the manner in which the bleeding was produced and its origin than would have been the case on a normal skin. The appearance of the left hand remained up to 1 a.m. essentially the same as I had found it on Thursday. At midnight I observed a possibly rather humid reflection of the wound, but the bad light and the already shiny aspect of the wound prevented me from making sure of this.

Besides, continuous observation was made quite impossible. Therese often lifted the bed-coverings very high in front of her, and the only time on such an occasion that we tried to approach the head of the bed, with Professor Killermann, the angry protest of the father at once obliged us to withdraw. During these intervals – when the parents explained that Therese needed to fan herself – I was struck by the strange and very intense movements Therese made with her arms and legs, movements which for the sole purpose of fanning herself were ample beyond measure and left me with a very bad impression.

As all the time I had seen only 'stagnant blood', and had never been able to see it bleeding from the eyes and hands, I made it my duty, from 2 am, to attend particularly to this bleeding. My conviction that I must here be on my guard was strengthened by the insistence with which Therese assured us several times after 2.50 am, that we could go home, 'because there would be no more till five o'clock', and then, when at 3.50 am they made us – Professor Stöckl and myself – leave the room for some minutes, it was precisely during this interval that a copious bleeding took place. As my report shows, the united efforts of myself and the other members of the commission were rendered useless, because on two occasions (between 8.10 and 8.25 and about 11.30), all the observers were made to leave the room precisely at the moment when, as was afterwards established, a fresh effusion of blood covered the dried scabs.

I never succeeded in seeing the wound on the breast nor that on the scalp. It goes without saying that in these conditions there could be no question of an exact observation of the 'bleedings'. The fact that two or three times the observers were made to go out just at the moment when a fresh effusion of blood evidently came to cover the wounds arouses the suspicion, on the contrary, that during this time something happened which needed to be hidden from observation. It was for the same reason that I disliked her frequent manipulations behind the raised coverings.[11]

Clearly then, while Therese Neumann cannot be proved a fraud, this investigation does not inspire any degree of confidence in her.

Around this time there were undoubted attempts to fake stigmata. This is clear from another German case, that of Paul Diebel, who in 1928 arrived in Paris claiming to be able to cry tears of blood at will, and to produce other stigmata. Unfortunately for Diebel, he more than met his match in a physician called Dr Osty who, on turning back Diebel's eyelids, revealed that the conjunctivae had been carefully pricked by a needle. Similarly Diebel had made scratches on the inner part of his thighs so that, if he kept his legs tightly pressed together, he could surreptitiously squeeze out enough blood from these to fake bleeding from his hands.

But if all this might seem highly discouraging to there being anything genuine to the stigmatic phenomenon, against this must not only be balanced the already mentioned direct eyewitness accounts of spontaneous bleedings, and the rigorous tests on Louise Lateau, but also more recent if less well-known stigmatic cases.

One such has been that of a little-known Englishwoman, Dorothy Kerin, who between 1902 and 1912 was so severely stricken with what her doctors diagnosed as tuberculosis that by the evening of 18 February 1912 she was adjudged to be within a whisker of death, even though she was only twenty-one. Then, with some sixteen of her closest friends and relatives gathered sorrowfully in her bedroom in Herne Hill, London, she staged an apparent recovery every bit as dramatic as that of Bertha Mrazek. Hearing a voice tell her to 'get up and walk', she did just that, despite having been bed-ridden for some five years, and then, to her on-lookers amazement, went on to eat a hearty meal.

Similarly strikingly reminiscent of Bertha Mrazek three years later, after reporting a variety of visions of Jesus and the Virgin Mary, Dorothy went on to manifest her stigmata. The afternoon of the Feast of the Immaculate Conception, while staying at the Enfield home of Anglican vicar Dr Langford-James, she complained of intense pains, particularly in her left hand, whereupon, while Dr Langford-James watched, a red spot gradually appeared on the back of this, followed shortly after by a matching wound in the palm. The next day, as she knelt kissing the feet of a crucifix, she felt more intense pains, then two stabs as if from a knife, whereupon, just like Padre Pio, she fainted. On coming to, she found that wounds had now appeared in her left side, and in her right hand, to be followed the next day by wounds in her feet.

Although regrettably no-one seems to have taken photographs, Dr Langford-James at least lost no time summoning independent witnesses, urging them to set down in writing what they observed.

According to one, the Rev Austen Taylor of Walthamstow:

> She [Dorothy Kerin] . . . allowed me to see and examine her
> hands. In both there was a wound right through the palm.
> In one the colour was a much deeper black-red (the colour of
> clotted blood) than the other; in the darker one something like
> a nailhead seemed to be coming away. Dr Langford-James,
> who was present, then obtained permission to uncover the
> feet. There, also, in both feet showing through from the upper
> side to the sole, were the wounds, in that part of the foot which
> is flexible just below the arch.[12]

Without any suggestion of either exhibitionism or fraudulence
Dorothy Kerin retained the wounds for some ten years, and went
on later in life to found the still extant Burrswood healing centre,
where she died in 1963.

Another modern case, this time, rather better than that of
Dorothy Kerin, observed under scientifically controlled conditions
by qualified medical practitioners, has been that of Canadian
housewife Mrs Eva McIsaac, born in 1902 in the tiny village of
Uptergrove between Lakes Simcoe and Couchiching some eighty
miles north of Ontario. The grand-daughter of a full-blooded
Huron Indian, Eva showed little aptitude for school, and on marrying Uptergrove farmer Donald McIsaac, concentrated all her efforts
on rearing eight children, two of whom sadly died in infancy.
A devout Roman Catholic, Eva attended Mass every day, but
otherwise her life seemed unremarkable.

Then in 1937 she reportedly experienced a vision, followed by
the appearance of a small painful sore on the back of her right
hand, which as subsequently became evident, was the onset of
stigmata. Eva at first tried to hide this, but once her family saw
it they insisted she visit a doctor, the first of several who proved
unable to persuade the sore to heal.

In the years leading up to 1940 she became much more explicitly
stigmatised, a side-wound manifesting and becoming particularly
deep and painful, the wounds in her hands penetrating deeper
until they seemed to reach through to her palms, and those in
her feet to the soles. A Protestant medical specialist who studied
her reported:

> The wounds are most peculiar. Those on the hands and feet
> are square. On the backs of the hands and on the insteps they
> are dark and slightly hard. On the palms and the soles they

are somewhat smaller and rather reddish in colour and are covered with a sort of transparent tissue. The wound in the left side is deep and shaped like a long narrow diamond. On the head under the hairline there are numerous small wounds, mostly circular in shape. On the back there are several crosswise reddish marks, rather like lash marks.[13]

Like those of Domenica Lazzari, Therese Neumann and others, Eva's wounds gradually settled into a pattern of manifesting on Fridays. They remained visible but dry and pain-free during the rest of the week, but on Friday evenings between six and nine they flared up with such intensity that some witnesses are said to have fainted. The wounds would also apparently bleed between 11 pm on Maundy Thursday and midnight on Good Friday, and around this time she also suffered a 'carrying of the cross' wound on her right shoulder which bled on Good Friday, becoming what one Catholic physician described as 'an immense bleeding wound'. Yet it had healed by Easter Sunday.

Despite very modest financial circumstances, Eva appears to have shunned monetary and other inducements to make her an object of public spectacle, and to have avoided giving interviews to journalists. More importantly, she freely made herself available for intensive medical examinations. One of these, in 1945, lasted three weeks. Another was for two weeks in 1946, at St Michael's Hospital and Bresica Hall in Ontario.

Such was the thoroughness and intensity of these that she was not left alone for a single moment, day or night. Blood samples were taken during her Friday agonies and on ordinary days. She had no clock or watch in her room, and her mealtimes were surreptitiously advanced in order that she should have a mistaken idea of the true time. Despite this, her agonies still began at 6 pm and continued until 9 pm. A Protestant doctor who was one of her observers described the scene:

> Mrs McIsaac was bright, lively and full of energy right up until late Friday afternoon . . . During the early part of the week she was in very good health despite the marks . . . perfectly normal except that she is fairly deaf and has weak eyes . . . She talked easily and cheerfully. She talked a good deal about her religion, in which she is obviously a devout believer, but she also talked of other things.
>
> On Friday afternoon the marks on her body began to lose their hardness, and towards six o'clock they appeared more

like fresh wounds. It was apparent that she was beginning to
feel pain . . . She appeared to lapse into a trance . . . Her pain
seemed to intensify to agony . . . Then a minute drop of blood
appeared at the hairline . . . Soon a drop of blood began to form
at one of the foot wounds . . . Gradually the hands and the
other wounds began to bleed. The wounds on the back bled
only a few drops . . . The others bled a good deal . . . By nine
o'clock her face was covered in blood from the head wounds
and her hair was matted with it.[14]

Whatever the suspicions we may harbour concerning Bertha
Mrazek and Therese Neumann, here we have a direct attestation
of stigmatic wounds manifesting spontaneously under controlled
conditions. The medical reports of Eva's accompanying psychological behaviour reveal such similarities with other stigmatics that
the validity of all must for the present at least remain open. For
clearly, just like Elizabeth of Herkenrode, Lukardis of Oberweimar, and others from long before, Eva went into some form of
trance.

At times during this three-hour period she raised up to a sitting
position . . . stretched her arms out in front of her . . . She did
not respond to questions during the times when she was
apparently in a coma . . . She was insensitive to the touch of
a hand or to a sudden noise . . .
  There were pauses during which the pain apparently
subsided. During these lapses she answered questions and
described what she had seen while in the comatose condition.
Though her eyes were open a match or a hand passed in front
of her eyes produced no reaction, no blinking . . . After each
pause the pain appeared to return more strongly. Her agony
intensified and the bleeding increased until she seemed to lapse
into complete unconsciousness.[15]

Eva McIsaac's case is not alone in such respects. Besides Jane
Hunt, with whom we began this book, the formal medical literature of recent years contains other little-known cases in which
spontaneous stigmatic bleeding has been reliably observed.
  For instance, from psychiatrist J. V. Hynes of the Royal Brisbane
Hospital, Australia, has come a report of reliably observed stigmata on the part of a Polish-born patient who had come into his
care, identified for reasons of medical confidentiality only as Mrs
H.[16] According to Dr Hynes, in 1958 Mrs H. suffered a serious
bite from a poisonous spider, and although she was swiftly dis-

charged from hospital, her behaviour from around this time became strange. On 23 May 1958 she experienced a vision of the Virgin Mary who told her she had to suffer for the sins of others, following which every Friday she passed into a trance-like state from which she could not be woken. She described pains in her arms and legs 'as if someone was twisting them' and often cried tears of blood.

These 'tears of blood' seem to have been Mrs H's particular brand of stigmata, and they were observed by her local physician, a Dr F. and also by his wife. Dr Hynes reported:

> On Thursday nights she was restless and slept badly. On Friday mornings she bathed, dressed herself in a white nightdress, and put clean linen on her bed in which she lay holding a fresh handkerchief in her hand. Then, following a series of writhing movements, she passed into a trance state when she became impervious to all external stimuli, including pain. During this period she claimed to have visions of the Virgin Mary, and sometimes of St Francis of Assisi. On many Fridays, at about 4.45 pm, blood appeared below her closed eyelids, forming brown crusts which she would wipe away with her handkerchief when she returned to normal consciousness. Mrs F. [the doctor's wife] who witnessed the bleeding on at least six occasions, wiped away the blood with cotton wool, leaving a clear unmarked skin beneath the crusts. Within two minutes blood reappeared on the lower lids, the whole phenomenon persisting for about fifteen minutes. Both Dr and Mrs F. were satisfied that the blood did not originate from her conjunctivae but oozed through the intact skin of her lower eyelids. Probably it originated from sweat ducts for, on wiping away the blood, the skin was free of all marks or bruising such as might have been expected if the blood had come from broken blood vessels or an open lesion. There is no evidence that the bleeding was self-induced and at no time was she observed touching her eyelids with her hands.[17]

Similar directly-witnessed bleeding also features in a more recent case, that of Cloretta Robinson, a black girl from West Oakland, California. Cloretta began bleeding from the palm of her left hand while sitting in her school classroom on 17 March 1972, then at irregular intervals during the subsequent nineteen days up to the Good Friday. As scrupulously recorded by Dr Laretta

F. Early of the Department of Pediatrics, West Oakland Health Center, California, who directly studied her case:

[Cloretta] bled from the right palm on the fourth day, from the dorsum of the left foot on the sixth day, from the dorsum of the right foot and the right thorax on the seventh day, and from the middle of her forehead on the fourteenth day, seven days before Easter Sunday. For a total of nineteen days various persons and the patient [i.e. Cloretta] reported bleeding from these sites, usually one to five times daily, but with the frequency decreasing to once every two days. She bled from the hands more frequently than from the other sites. Numerous instances of blood appearing at the previously mentioned sites were observed by her school teachers, the school nurse, nurse's assistant, physician [i.e. Dr Early] and on one occasion other hospital staff.

Numerous instances of the blood appearing were observed by family members only, e.g. the one occasion when blood appeared on her forehead. The family took photographs of the drops of blood on the forehead; some of these photographs were later distributed to inquiring newspaper reporters and were widely printed accompanying news accounts. The school nurse, while holding her hand on one occasion, noted blood forming on the palm . . .

On her fourth appointment she spent four hours in the physician's office with two other observers in an attempt to photograph the bleeding, but none occurred that day. Near noon the following day she returned to the office; after talking with her for about one half-hour the physician suggested that she sit in the examination room next to her office and draw pictures of St Francis of Assisi from a book she had brought with her. The patient was alone, as nursing staff was on lunch break, and while copying pictures she started bleeding from her left palm. She immediately returned to the physician's office with two to three drops of blood in the palm of her left hand. The physician observed the blood to increase in volume four-fold, welling up from the centre of the palm and spreading over the palmar creases.[18]

And before he had come across present-day British stigmatic Jane Hunt, journalist Ted Harrison, who wrote and narrated the programme about her, had earlier witnessed stigmatic wounds developing on another British case, that of Ethel Chapman, a woman patient in a Leonard Cheshire home, whose hand wounds erupted even while Harrison was interviewing her for a radio programme. The following is a transcript of that interview:

Harrison: May I have a look at your hands, Ethel. Just off centre of the palms you have two scars, two marks, and on your left hand there's been some recent movement, some recent bleeding. The other side of your hand, if I can just turn them over, Ethel, there's another mark which corresponds as if a nail has gone through . . . At the moment it looks as if there's a fairly new mark on the surface of your right hand, on the top. Has that been bleeding at all, Ethel?

Ethel Chapman: Oh yes, I hadn't noticed . . . It wasn't when I came down. I'm pretty sure.

Harrison: I didn't notice it.

Ethel Chapman: No, I didn't notice it.

Harrison: And your left hand is still unmarked though perhaps just . . .

Ethel Chapman: Just a little.

Harrison: Part of the skin seems to have just scraped away on the top.

Ethel Chapman: Yes . . .

Harrison: Can I look at the other side again, Ethel? There doesn't seem to be a mark, except on the left hand. Again there's a . . .

Ethel Chapman: That's a new one, yes. And there's one coming in the same place there.

Harrison: Can you actually see it? Can you see if the skin is breaking?

Ethel Chapman: I think it has broken, or is on the verge.

Harrison: Do you know the moment at which it is going to break?

Ethel Chapman: Usually, I get a little pin-prick feeling. This time I haven't.

Harrison: It's more active again now. There's a mark that's just at the base of the scar on the inside of your left palm. It's a lot newer than just a few seconds ago. It's as if the skin is breaking, because earlier on I remember this was a distinct area of fairly old scab mark, wasn't it?

Ethel Chapman: Yes.[19]

Ted Harrison, highly respected for his BBC religious programmes, subsequently affirmed:

I can say . . . that her wounds changed their state during the course of an interview. The change was very slight but quite noticeable . . . It was not . . . due to her rubbing the wounds, scratching them or picking them either with her own hands or an instrument.[20]

So despite the need for continuing vigilance against fraud, it can be said with confidence that in the case of some, if not all, claimed stigmatics their flesh does seem spontaneously to change and bleed in the same manner as has been reported even since the time of St Francis. Besides those already remarked on, other stigmatics are still active. They include Roberto Casarin of Turin, who on Good Friday 1983, at the age of eighteen, exhibited a bloody cross on his forehead just as was reported of Soeur Jeanne des Anges at Loudun back in the seventeenth century; retired hospital porter Salvatore Marchese of Sicily, whose wounds break out beneath heavily bandaged hands, and who has been credited with several apparent healings; and not least the blind and heretical Spanish Archbishop Clemente Dominguez, whose well-photographed stigmata include a particularly livid wound in the side and bleedings as from a crown of thorns on his forehead.

So what is happening? What strange psychology seems to inform stigmatic after stigmatic? It is to these fundamental questions that our attention must now be directed.

WHAT MANNER OF WOUNDS?

IF we now guardedly accept that at least some stigmatics' wounds seem to be spontaneous, it is clearly important that we look in more detail at what is happening at the physical level. A priority is to establish a clear clinical picture of the stigmatic.

For instance, is there any significant predisposition to becoming a stigmatic on the part of one sex or the other? There has been a marked tendency for the phenomenon to predominate among women, despite the fact that the greatest and least contested stigmatics, Padre Pio and St Francis of Assisi, were both male. Dr Imbert-Goubeyre's nineteenth century census lists only forty-one men compared to 280 women, a ratio of one to seven, and despite certain limitations to his researches, there is every justification for believing such a proportion to be a reliable enough guide.

Another key question is whether there is any preferential age at which stigmatics first receive their wounds? Here the pattern is not so clear. Domenica Lazzari was nineteen, Marie-Julie Jahenny was twenty, Dorothy Kerin twenty-six, Therese Neumann and Jane Hunt both twenty-eight, Padre Pio thirty-one, Eva McIsaac thirty-five, and St Francis of Assisis forty-two. But back in the sixteenth century Francesca de Serrone manifested her wound in the side at the age of only fourteen. In the seventeenth century Angela della Pace became stigmatised at the age of nine. In the eighteenth century French girl Madeleine Morice first received her wounds at the age of eight. And in our own time the young American Baptist girl Cloretta Robinson began her bleedings at the age of eleven.

Similarly there is no evidence of any upper age limit or cut-off stage. In the seventeenth century the Sicilian nun Delicia di Giovanni's first wound appeared on her right hand when she was sixty-five, with further ones appearing each year until she was seventy. In the nineteenth century the French lay stigmatic Jeanne Boisseau's wounds also appeared at the age of sixty-five, reportedly accompanied by particularly vigorous bleeding. And Padre Pio's wounds, although beginning when he was thirty-one, continued seemingly unabated right up to the time of his death fifty years later.

Next needs to be considered what can be determined of the distribution of the wounds over each stigmatic's body. Although not all stigmatics have manifested a full complement of crucifixion-type wounds (the thirteenth century Dominican nun Emilia Piccheri had only a crown of thorns and two seventeenth century nuns had only a side-wound) an important consideration is whether or not the same wounds have mostly appeared in the same locations. The crux here is that if every stigmatic, or even a significant proportion of them, manifested their wounds in the same places on their bodies, and with the same shapes, then even if there were differences of degree it could be argued that all were replications of a single pattern, namely Jesus Christ's crucifixion injuries as he historically suffered them. From this we would have at least prima facie evidence for the wounds' divine origin.

But complicating the issue is that we have no certain knowledge of the precise locations of Jesus's crucifixion wounds. Was he, as imagined by most artists, nailed through the centre of each palm, or, as suggested by the controversial Holy Shroud of Turin, through the wrists? Was the lance plunged through his chest on his right side, or his left? At what level of his rib-cage did the lance penetrate? On which shoulder did he carry the cross? Even the information that Jesus was nailed rather than tied to the cross can only be inferred from the post-crucifixion words of St Thomas: 'Unless I see the holes that the nails made in his hands . . . I refuse to believe.'[1] Because of the vagueness of the gospels on such questions, and the absence of any other reliable source, we can only acknowledge our ignorance.

But quite aside from the question of where Jesus's own wounds were located, the sum total of the information we have about stigmatics' wounds indicates no consistency even remotely suggesting them as replications of one single, original pattern. Thus while most stigmatics have manifested their nail wounds in the

63

middle of their palms, the form of these wounds has varied markedly. Some have had slits in the palms, others mere round indentations, others almost unbroken skin. Likewise the wounds on the backs of the hands have varied, with some, such as those of Therese Neumann, even changing from round to rectangular. One little-known present-day stigmatic, Brother Gino Burresi of Rome, is said to exhibit the nail wounds in his wrists, in conformity with the location now most favoured from medical experiments,[2] from archaeological discoveries,[3] and from the Turin Shroud.

Similarly, there have been marked variations in the location of the side-wound. St Francis of Assisi, Blessed Dodo of Hascha and the Spanish Archbishop Clemente Dominguez all bore their wounds on the right side. But Padre Pio bore his on his left, as did Dorothy Kerin and Therese Neumann (although she claimed in her visions to have seen it on Jesus's right). According to Dr Imbert-Goubeyre's census, among twenty-eight stigmatics in whom the location of the side-wound is known, twenty-two featured it on the left compared to only six on the right; some bore it over their heart or opposite the heart, while others sported it almost under the arm.

There have been equally marked disparities in the shape of the side-wound. St Francis's was reported to have resembled 'an unhealed lance-wound'.[4] The photographs of Archbishop Clemente Dominguez and, for what they are worth, Bertha Mrazek, similarly show a lateral slit. The eighteenth century Swiss nun Maria-Josepha Kümi as well as Padre Pio are reliably reported to have had side-wounds in the form of a cross. Therese Neumann's was apparently cresent-shaped, Catherine Emmerich's was in the form of a Y, while others have featured a straight cut or even a triangle. And of the comparatively few who manifested 'carrying of the cross' wounds, some have featured these on the right shoulder, others on the left.

What of the pathological characteristics of the wounds? Here, while the clinical picture is again diverse, it is nonetheless intriguing, particularly so in respect of the most authoritative reports of the onset of the stigmata. Thus in the last century one of Louise Lateau's observers, Dr Gerald Molloy, wrote of her:

> There is no wound properly so-called, but the blood seems to force its way through the unbroken skin.[5]

This accords extraordinarily well with other descriptions. For instance, writing of the nineteenth century stigmatic St Gemma

Galgani, her biographer Padre Germano has told of her being visited on Friday by a doctor while she was bleeding and in one of her visionary states:

> The doctor took a towel, dipped it in water, and wiped Gemma's hands and forehead. The blood immediately disappeared and the skin showed no signs of cicatrix, scratch or puncture, as if there had never been any laceration.[6]

This recalls the case of the Polish-born Australian Mrs H. described in the last chapter:

> Mrs F. [the doctor's wife] who witnessed the bleeding on at least six occasions, wiped away the blood with cotton wool, leaving a clear unmarked skin beneath the crusts. Within two minutes blood reappeared on the lower lids... Both Doctor and Mrs F. were satisfied that the blood did not originate from her conjunctivae, but oozed through the intact skin of her lower eyelids... on wiping away the blood, the skin was free of all marks or bruising such as might have been expected if the blood had come from broken blood vessels or an open lesion.[7]

Corresponding equally closely are the clinical observations on Californian eleven-year-old Cloretta Robinson:

> The school nurse, while holding her hand on one occasion, noted blood forming on the palm. After wiping the palm, no fresh blood formed. She also examined the palm with a ten-power magnifying lens and found no lesions... while copying pictures she started bleeding from her left palm. She immediately returned to the physician's office with two or three drops of blood in the palm of her left hand. The physician observed the blood to increase in volume four-fold, welling up from the centre of the palm and spreading over the palmar creases. After wiping the wet blood away no lesions were present with the exception of a pea-size bluish discoloration remaining in the palm of her hand for approximately three minutes.[8]

Without, as far as I know, any awareness of any of these medical reports, Jane Hunt described to me the onset of her bleeding in almost identical terms:

> It just started seeping through the skin. There was no holes, or anything to speak of. It were just seeping through the skin.[9]

65

Such descriptions lead us to recall our earlier discussion of the case of the sixteenth century Portuguese stigmatic Maria de la Visitacion, whose wounds were declared fake because the Inquisition were able to scrub them clean. Might she have been genuine after all?

Equally striking are the accounts of the further development of the wounds. The next stage is apparently one of blistering. As Dr Lefebvre described during the course of his intensive investigation of Louise Lateau:

> On each of the reddish surfaces of the hands and feet a blister is seen to appear and gradually rise; when it is fully developed it forms a rounded, hemispheric protrusion on the surface of the skin; its base is of the same dimensions as the reddish surface on which it rests, that is, about two and a half centimetres long and one and a half wide . . . This blister is full of limpid serum. However, it often takes the colour of a more or less dark red on the palms of the hands and the soles of the feet . . . The zone of skin surrounding the blister is not the seat of any turgescence or reddening. [10]

A generation later Padre Germano similarly reported of St Gemma Galgani:

> Red marks showed themselves on the backs and palms of both hands; and under the epidermis a rent in the flesh was seen to open by degrees; this was oblong on the backs of the hands and irregularly round in the palms. After a little the membrane burst and on those innocent hands were seen marks of flesh wounds. The diameter of these in the palms was about half an inch, and on the backs of the hands the wound was about five eighths of an inch long by one eighth wide. [11]

As Jane Hunt described her wounds to me:

> Then they started going like volcanoes . . . sort of blistering up, but it wasn't a blister, sort of started going up in a lump until they'd explode. [12]

This inevitably leads to the product of that 'explosion', the onset of bleeding proper. Not least among the astonishing features of stigmatics' wounds is the amount of blood they have been claimed to discharge, along with, at times, peculiar accompaniments. As early as the Renaissance period Italian stigmatic Clare de Bugny is said to have amazed the professors of the Padua School of Medicine by the sheer volume of blood which poured from her side-wound, and by the perfume this exhaled. A few decades later the Franciscan nun Francesca de Serrone reportedly gushed forth blood from her side-wound so hot that it cracked the earthenware bowl in which it was being collected.

Louise Lateau was estimated to lose 250 grammes – approximately half a pint – of blood during one of her bleedings, Padre Pio about a cupful a day, and Jane Hunt, according to her own estimate, about a pint or a pint and a half. Although these are all estimates, they all indicate blood in profusion. Disappointingly few blood analyses appear to have been performed, but at least Louise Lateau's was confirmed as normal blood, though containing a higher than normal count of white corpuscles as she suffered from chloroanaemia.

But what of the fissures from which this blood came, when opened to their full extent? Could there have been actual penetration of the hands and feet, in the manner of a real nailing? In at least some well-attested instances this indeed appears to have been the case.

Regarding the eighteenth century Italian stigmatic St Maria Francesca of the Five Wounds, her confessor, Don Paschal Nitti, attested under oath during the proceedings for her beatification:

> As the apostle St Thomas did, (I) have put in my finger into
> the wounds of her hands and I have seen that the hole
> extended right through, for in inserting my first finger into the
> wound it met the thumb which I held underneath on the other
> side of the hand. And this experiment I have made in many
> Lents, and on many Fridays in March, because it was on such
> days that she said wounds were most fully developed.[13]

In the case of St Gemma Galgani, her biographer Padre Germano reported:

> Sometimes the laceration appeared to be only on the surface . . .
> but as a rule it was very deep and seemed to pass through
> the hand, the openings on both sides reaching each other. I
> say seemed to pass, because those cavities were full of blood,
> partly flowing and partly congealed, and when the blood
> ceased to flow they closed immediately, so that it was not easy
> to sound them without a probe.[14]

Almost exactly the same observation was made of Padre Pio by his physician Dr Romanelli:

I have a conviction amounting to certitude that the wounds are not superficial. Pressing on the palm with the thumb, one has the impression of a void. When thus pressing, it has not been possible to feel whether the wounds were joined together, for strong pressure causes the subject intense pain. I repeated the painful experiment, however, several times, both morning and evening, and must admit that I always came to the same conclusion.'[15]

Corroborating Dr Romanelli, Padre Pio's Father Provincial averred that he would be prepared to attest under oath that he could actually see through the holes in Padre Pio's hands.[16] And even in the case of Jane Hunt, when her hands were held up to the light, the tissue was observed to be peculiarly transparent. And she personally told me that the fissuring could sometimes be very deep.

But of all the features of stigmatics' wounds, perhaps the most incredible are the accounts, from as early as St Francis, of stigmatics apparently forming from within the wounds features in the likeness of crucifixion nails. The writers of the *Fioretti* reported of the nail wounds of St Francis:

His hands and feet appeared to have been pierced through the centre by nails, the heads of which were in the palms of his hands and the soles of his feet, standing out from the flesh; and their points issued from the backs of the hands and feet, so that they seemed to have been bent back and clinched in such a fashion that a finger could easily have been thrust through the bend outside the flesh as though a ring; and the heads of the nails were round and black.[17]

That this was not a mere late accretion to the story is evident from the fact that a portrait of St Francis painted within ten years of his death seems to show precisely one such nail.[18] Also a Bull of 1255, issued by Pope Alexander IV, remarks of him:

In his hands and in his feet he had most certainly nails, well-formed, of his own flesh, or of a substance newly produced.[19]

St Francis's biographer St Bonaventure described the same feature:

The clinched portion of the nails beneath the feet was so prominent, and projected so far, that not only did it prevent the soles from being set down freely upon the ground, but a finger on one's hand could easily be inserted in the bend under their curved extremities. So . . . I myself heard from those who had seen them with their own eyes.[20]

Had this phenomenon been observed only of St Francis, we might dismiss it as incredible. But it has been reported of stigmatics right up to our own time. One of the witnesses for the beatification of Giovanna Maria Bonomi, who died in 1670, attested that 'the flesh of her hands stood out like the head of a nail.'[21]

Of the nineteenth century Tyrolean stigmatic Domenica Lazzari, the medical specialist Dr Dei Cloche reported:

About the centre of the exterior of her hands, that is to say between the metacarp of the centre finger and the fourth, there rose a black spot resembling the head of a large nail, the diameter of which was just over an inch [nine lines in Italian measurement] and the form perfectly round.[22]

Similar remarks were made of St Gemma Galgani by Padre Germano:

The wounds in the palms of her hands were covered by a swelling that at first looked like clotted blood, whereas it was found to be fleshy, hard and like the head of a nail, raised and detached and about an inch in diameter.[23]

Of Dorothy Kerin, Brother William of Pershore Abbey, who witnessed her stigmata on 26 May 1917, reported:

The marks in Miss Kerin's hands and feet are . . . as though pierced by the holy nails, bearing the impress of the head of same in the palms of her hands and the instep of her feet, and the instep of her feet and the sharp point on the backs of her hands and the soles of her feet.[24]

And witness the following description of Therese Neumann's hand-wounds, as recorded by Dr Louis of Versailles:

On the back of the left hand I see a nail head, rectangular in shape, slightly longer than broad, in line with the hand. The rectangle it forms may be fifteen millimetres by ten; its edges are fined down and almost sharp, like those of an iron nail forged on the anvil. The mass of the nail-head is slightly convex, rounded in dome-shape. It shows numerous planes, not defined, like those produced by the blows of a smith's

69

hammer on a piece of ironwork. The colour is a reddish brown, like an ancient wax seal.[25]

According to a Dr van de Elst,' similar nail-heads were visible on Therese Neumann's feet:

> From the point of view of the shape, these . . . are curious in this respect that they appear as if chiselled by a cunning jeweller, with planes of extraordinary precision.[26]

However much we may feel obliged to distrust Therese Neumann on the overall evidence, it is a fact that a mid-life photograph of her very clearly shows the backs of both her hands with an unnaturally rectangular 'nail-head' exactly corresponding with these descriptions.[27]

Just as stigmatic wounds tend to open in a manner quite different from normal physical wounds, so they seem to close equally enigmatically. In the case of Gemma Galgani, for instance, however deep the fissuring of her Friday wounds, during the subsequent days those would disappear, leaving the skin just whitish. In the case of Louise Lateau, after her Friday stigmatisations the blood would again dry. Then, in the words of Dr Imbert-Goubeyre:

> On Saturday the stigmata of the day before gradually wither and dry up; on the three following days only stains remain.[28]

In the case of St Francis and Padre Pio, their wounds seem to have remained more or less consistently open, but other stigmatics have often manifested themselves on specific days, after which the wounds disappear or dry up. A common day for wounds to manifest was Friday. This was the case with Lukardis of Oberweimar, St Catherine de Ricci, Francesca de Serrone, Domenica Lazzari, Louise Lateau, St Gemma Galgani and Eva McIsaac. Often the timing of the wounds' onset would be very precise. Mrs McIsaac always manifested between 6 pm and 9 pm, despite attempts to confuse her by altering clocks and meal times. Other stigmatics, like Jane Hunt, have had 'special day' manifestations, Easter being a favoured time. Also deserving of mention are those whose wounds have manifested and ceased according to their own prediction, as for instance the seventeenth century Veronica Giuliani, who prophesied that her stigmata would last three years, which they did, and Marie-Julie Jahenny, who similarly predicted when her various wounds and blemishes would appear and disappear.

In the case of St Gemma Galgani her wounds could on occasion be commanded to open or close at the instigation of her confessor. As she described in her *Relation*:

> There were times when the father Confessor said to me: 'How long will the perforation in the side remain open?' I replied: 'Our Lord seems to wish it should remain open for so many hours or days' according as I had been given to understand, and exactly at that time it would close again. But sometimes he (the Confessor) said to me: 'I do not wish it to close before such a day or such an hour.' And in fact it would happen so . . . If I am not mistaken the Bishop on one occasion did the same thing. He came here with certain of God's servants and they wished to see this wound in the side open, to my great sorrow. Then the Bishop told me that he would come again the next day but wished the wound to be closed. And so precisely it came about.[29]

The whole phenomenon is undeniably bizarre, and yet the observations are too persistent and too consistent for it all to be dismissed as make-believe. Despite popular belief, it seems from the diversity of the wounds' locations and shapes most unlikely that any are actual replications of the original Crucifixion injuries. Nonetheless, stigmata are still of profound interest in themselves. For if the flesh really does change, why should it do so among this such a select band of people? Exactly how does it occur, and what triggers it off? It is obvious that instead of finding answers, we are only beginning to ask the right questions.

OF VISIONS AND VOICES

IF, in the light of what we have seen so far, we try to establish what type of person becomes a stigmatic, one of the first and most obvious features is that the individual tends to be religious, and often has chosen a religious vocation.

Dr Imbert-Goubeyre's census shows that well over two thirds of his 321 cases had taken religious vows. His list comprised 109 Dominicans, 102 Franciscans (a quarter of these Poor Clare nuns), fourteen Carmelite friars or nuns, fourteen Ursulines, twelve Visitation nuns, eight Augustinians, three Jesuits and a miscellany of others. The list is of interest as much for those religious orders that have gone unrepresented as for those that it includes. Why do we look in vain for the great, ancient and numerous Benedictine and Cistercian orders? Why so few Jesuits? And even allowing that St Francis was the first stigmatic, why such a preponderance of Franciscans and Dominicans?

At this stage we still know far too little to answer such questions directly. What does seem to emerge is that stigmatics tend to come from those orders laying their greatest accent on personal austerity and the contemplative life. This impression becomes reinforced when we note that of the lay stigmatics on Dr Imbert-Goubeyre's list, a large number have combined some form of affectation of piety with long periods bedridden as a result of some serious illness, real or imaginary.

So could long drawn out mental dwelling on Jesus's Passion and Crucifixion have some bearing on the manifestation of stigmata? That this factor must be significant becomes evident from even a perfunctory review of the circumstances in which each stigmatic received his or her wounds. What was St Francis involved in before the sudden onset of his bleeding? The tradition is clear: he was ecstatically caught up in a vision of the crucified Jesus. What brought on the stigmata of Lukardis of Oberweimar? She had a vision of a young man bearing Christ-like wounds, who pressed his bleeding hand against hers with the words: 'I want you to suffer along with me.' How did Catherine Emmerich first receive her forehead stigmata? According to her own account:

> I saw my Divine Spouse under the form of a young man, gloriously aureoled in radiant light, come towards me . . . in his right (hand) a crown of thorns.[1]

How did Domenica Lazzari receive her wounds of the same kind? According to what she told her family:

> During the night a very beautiful lady came to my bedside and set a crown upon my head.[2]

Even a twentieth century British stigmatic, the late Ethel Chapman, told interviewers:

> I thought it was a dream, I felt myself being drawn onto the cross. I felt the pain of the nails through my hands and through my feet. . . . I could see the crowds all jeering and shouting. . . . When the nurses came to bath me and wash me they noticed my hands were bleeding.[3]

Similarly, Jane Hunt had a vision of Jesus, then the very next morning blood began pouring from the centre of her palms. In fact, whenever we have detailed information about the onset of stigmata, almost invariably the stigmatic is reported experiencing some form of vision either before or during the bleeding itself.

Is it really credible that visions could be responsible for such powerful flesh changes? In this regard it is important that we forget the sanitised visitations that so often comprise the traditional 'vision' as portrayed in television and cinema religious epics. Instead, it is quite evident from the convulsive exhibitions of some of the earliest stigmatics, such as Elizabeth of Herkenrode and Lukardis of Oberweimar, that their experiences have been inward dramas of extraordinary and physically all-consuming intensity.

St Maria Maddalena de' Pazzi shocked her convent sisters by the sheer ardour with which she received her visions of Jesus:

O Lord, my God, it is enough, it is too much, O Jesus . . . O God of Love, no, I can never stop from crying of love.[4]

However 'exaggerated' this might seem, it is evident that whoever recorded Maria Magdalena's words back in the sixteenth century was faithful to their flavour.

For there were equally intense outpourings and writhings on the part of English stigmatic Teresa Higginson, carefully recorded by her friend Susan Ryland as they happened before her eyes during Holy Week in 1874. The following are from Miss Ryland's notes of Teresa's apparent viewing of the abuses suffered by Jesus immediately prior to his Crucifixion:

Sees him [Jesus] bound in the garden, stretches out her hands and begs to be bound instead. Blow on right cheek by the mouth. Blow on left eye. Heavy groans. A blow on mouth. Pulling of beard. Holds her chin. Low cries of pain. Sickness. A blow on left side of head. Beard is pulled. Turns aside in horror, gasps. Buffeted about the head. 'Canst thou stand with Him. Oh let me go with thee, Lord thou canst not bear it.' Writhes in fearful agony, apparently being scourged. Rests. A cry of pain, writhing again, rests, fearful writhing, rests. 'Oh see how torn he is, Ah find me something soft for mercy's sake.' Dreadful agony. Puts hand to head with a look of great pain. 'Oh put it on me, you have done enough.' Crowning with thorns. Groans and writhes and clenches her hands. Raises her hand to her head and then to left cheek in great pain. . . . 'Oh Lord they know not what they do.' Is quite still for three minutes. Sees the drink offered. 'Oh take it, Lord.' Calls out in agony. 'Oh stay him Lord.' Stretches out her hand for the cross. 'Oh Lord let me bear it a little while. Thou art too weak. Oh lean on me. Thou art too weak. Oh Jesus, lean.' First fall to the right. 'Oh Jesus let me raise thee.' A blow on left cheek. 'Oh Jesus let me raise thee.' A blow on left cheek. 'Stand back.' A blow on right cheek. 'Oh Mary. Oh Jesus! Support her. Oh Jesus, oh Mary!' Stripping off garments. Begs to be allowed to take them off. 'Oh, take them gently. Oh, pure God.' Appears to feel garments torn. Holds them at the waist. 'Oh holy and pure God. Most keenly felt by thee, oh my Jesus.' Turns her head aside in anguish. Moans. 'I will not let thee go' . . .[5]

Evident from this, and typically stigmatic, is Teresa's constantly shifting role from being a sympathetic bystander, to being 'inside' Jesus and feeling all his sufferings within her own body. Some fifty years later, in Konnersreuth, similar first-hand observations were made by Therese Neumann's visions by Monsignor Kaspar, Bishop of Königgrätz:

> How striking Therese's appearance now! She suffers terribly. She looks to the right. She sees the clothes being torn from Jesus's body. She keeps looking to the right. She sees Jesus being nailed to the cross. From all his wounds the blood flows fresh and red. Heart-rending sight! She scarcely breathes. She moves her fingers, like Jesus when they nailed him to the cross. She suffers terribly: her whole body shudders, and her feet too (during the crucifixion). She clenches her hands, joins her feet, which tremble again, stretches her hands out to the Saviour, clutches with the fingers of her right hand and cries 'Oh!', then looks with terror on the scene before her. 'Oh!' She is rigid . . .[6]

Therese's biographer Anni Spiegl noted of similar performances:

> I had the opportunity of being with Therese on Fridays in Lent and on ordinary Fridays and was able to watch her closely. . . . The individual stations of the Passion could be recognised from Therese's facial expression. After the crowning with thorns she tried to pluck the thorns out of her head exactly in the places where there were bloodstains on the white kerchief. . . . Therese was angry with Simon because he took the cross so awkwardly and thus caused the Saviour to fall. . . . You could see Therese looking to the right and the left towards the two thieves, you saw her looking down to the mother of Christ at the foot of the cross. She suffered the terrible thirst too, and often experienced severe fits of choking at the crucifixion. . . .
> Therese was . . . in the land she saw with all her senses. You could see her shivering or feeling the heat, turning up her nose at unpleasant smells or sniffing with relish the aroma of herbs and ointments. Anyone who had the opportunity of watching Therese's facial expression during her visions can no longer have any doubts as to their authenticity. Joy, fear, amazement, inquisitiveness and horror passed over her face in turn within a matter of seconds. . . .[7]

While it might have looked convincing, a cold, hard question nonetheless needs to be asked. Were Teresa, Therese and all the other stigmatics viewing the events surrounding Jesus's crucifixion as they actually happened around 30 AD, or merely as they imagined them?

Just as the variety of stigmatics' wounds suggests they cannot all be exact replications of the wounds of Jesus, so an appraisal of stigmatics' visions fails to convince that any one of them has genuinely experienced a time-travel viewing of first century Jerusalem.

Among the best recorded visions, for instance, are those of the early nineteenth century German nun Catharine Emmerich. No less than four published volumes derive from the notes taken at her bedside by the poet Clemens Brentano,[8] with apparent insights into Jesus's last hours more vivid and intimate than anything to be found in the gospels. In these we follow the elaborate preparations and ceremonial for the Last Supper. We are accorded flowing descriptions of the judgment hall of Caiaphas and the palace of Pilate. Not a blow seems to be omitted from Jesus's savage scourging by six drunken and blood-thirsty sadists. We are told of housewife Veronica wiping Jesus's face with her veil. We learn how special holes had to be dug for the three crosses. And we grieve with the holy women as they wash Jesus's lifeless body and lavish it with unguents in preparation for his burial.

But it is precisely this welter of detail that gives rise to most disquiet. Just how satisfied can we be that her account of the Last Supper is authentic? Should we really believe her assertion that the Last Supper chalice once belonged to Abraham? Does her description of Caiaphas's mansion accord with modern excavations of the city's first century priestly dwellings? Is it not a little suspicious that the Veronica story as she describes it owes nothing to any original gospel and everything to medieval legend? Does her assertion that Adam was buried at Golgotha owe more to symbol-seeking tradition than accurate reportage? How sure can we be that Jesus's body was washed and anointed before burial? The gospels do not specifically say so, and according to some, when a Jew died a bloody death the religious requirement was that he should not be washed in order that his life's blood should be buried with him.

One could go into great detail on the way Catharine was anachronistic or just plain wrong on point after point of this kind. But perhaps more telling is the absence in her visions of any convincing 'period' feel, and the inclusion of many stories, like that of Veronica, difficult to accept as anything other than apocrypha.

We find exactly the same in the visions of other stigmatics. A vision of Mary Magdalen reportedly came to Therese Neumann while she was sitting on a sofa talking with her parish priest, Father Naber, and two other priests. This was described by one of those present:

> Therese saw how Magdalen, together with two other women
> and two men, were placed on a ship without sails or rudder
> and set adrift on the sea, destined to inevitable death. A storm
> arose, and Therese became filled with terror as she saw how
> the vessel was tossed about.[9]

Therese went on to mention how she also saw the cave where Mary Magdalen spent her last years, and how, peeping through a hole in the wall, she spied her as an old woman hovering in ecstasy above the ground shortly before her death.

This was just the sort of pious tale that Therese would have heard as part of her religious instruction. As has been pointed out by the Jesuit historian Revd Herbert Thurston:

> The story of the voyage of Saints Mary Magdalen, Lazarus,
> Martha and others across the Mediterranean, and of the long
> penance of the first named . . . is now completely discredited.
> The authoritative Catholic work of reference, the *Lexikon für
> Theologie und Kirche* . . . rejects the legend as 'altogether
> unhistorical'.[10]

Despite such arguments, it might be possible to hold a sympathetic view of stigmatic visions if they displayed details which could not normally have been known to the stigmatic. Several stigmatics, including Ethel Chapman, have reported that they could hear people in the vision speaking in their original languages. Few stigmatics have been able to repeat what they heard in this way, but one of whom this claim has been made was Therese Neumann. Therese, with her peasant upbringing, was never formally educated in any foreign or ancient language, yet her biographer Steiner states that among the languages she seemed able to hear were Aramaic, for example: 'Shelamlach, Miriam' (Hail Mary); Greek, for example:

> 'Zoslin' (They are alive! – the exclamation of the multitudes
> after John the Apostle had raised two dead men to life in
> Smyrna, a locale where Greek was spoken); and French: 'Mon

Dieu, je vous aime' (My God, I love you – words of the Little Flower [Thérèse of Lisieux] shortly before her death).[11]

In fact all this is much less impressive than at first appears. The 'je vous aime' quotation is scarcely beyond the wit even of the most unschooled in French, and Therese is also likely to have come across it in what she read of her French namesake and idol.

As for Aramaic, a high proportion of her words were those specifically recorded in the gospels, e.g. 'Kum' (Get up) in Mark 5:4, and 'Eloi, Eloi lama sabachthani' from Mark 15:34. But totally damning is the information from one of Therese's contemporaries that she only began using such words after she had acquired a tutor, one Dr Wutz. Professor Ewald, one of those who studied Therese, wrote:

Unfortunate from a scientific viewpoint, it seems to me, is the influence of another priest (viz. Dr Wutz), whom I do not wish to deny does it in good faith, but who visits her very frequently and in his high-spirited manner has without any doubt drummed a good deal into her. Thus, and only thus, can it be explained that Therese has of a sudden begun to hallucinate in Aramaic, while formerly the Saviour's words were given by her in good Upper Palatinate [i.e. Therese's own native German].[12]

An important pointer to what is happening lies in another phenomenon involving individuals appearing to re-experience the historical past – that of regression into so-called past lives or previous incarnations. Hypnotised subjects often behave convincingly when seeming to re-live some dramatic historical event from a supposed earlier incarnation. Famous cases have included American housewife Virginia Tighe 'regressing' to a life as nineteenth century Irish girl Bridey Murphy, and Welsh housewife Jane Evans who recalled no less than six previous existences, ranging from a tutor's wife living in fourth century Roman Britain, to a handmaid of Catherine of Aragon. Sometimes the detail can be remarkably impressive.

But as I have exhaustively shown elsewhere,[13] when these claims are properly scrutinised they fail to offer any serious case for believing the hypnotised individuals to have been transported back to the historical past. This is not to suggest any conscious fraudulence, either by the hypnotist or the hypnotised. What appears to happen is that when a hypnotised subject is asked to go back to times before he or she was born, long forgotten memories of stories or films read or viewed perhaps many years ago are re-activated, and re-lived as if they were real events. Nor is this mere hypothesis. Although it is a needle-in-a-haystack exercise, sometimes exact sources can be identified, as in the case of Jane Evans's apparent life in Roman Britain. This can be conclusively traced to her reading a particular historical novel, Louis de Wohl's *The Living Wood*, published in 1947 and set in Roman Britain during the early years of Emperor Constantine the Great. Not only did Jane's hypnotic memory include the real historical characters, such as Constantine and his mother Helena, but the fictional ones as well. The rare instances of 'regressed' individuals seeming to speak unlearned languages similarly turn out to have a rational explanation.

Time and again the influences on stigmatics can be traced to items of inspiration from their ordinary lives. Often it is possible for the sources to be directly identified. In the case of St Francis, for instance, we have already seen how at the very beginning of his calling to a life of sanctity it was a Byzantine crucifix hanging in the church of San Damiano that deeply affected him, to such an extent that he felt Christ spoke to him from it. When Padre Pio received his stigmatisation, it was while praying before a particularly realistic statuette of Jesus on the cross. In the case of Polish-born Mrs H., her Brisbane psychiatrists reported that her room:

> had more the semblance of a chapel then a place to sleep in.
> It contained four crucifixes and three holy pictures, whose
> positions on the walls she varied according to their
> appropriateness for certain days of the calendar. One picture,
> Veronica's Veil, may be particularly significant for the
> developments in this woman's religious life.[14]

Ethel Chapman freely acknowledged that prior to her visions and stigmatisation an evangelist called Fay Roberts, who regularly broadcast on Birkenhead hospital radio, had visited her and talked to her about Jesus's crucifixion. Ethel told interviewer Ted Harrison:

> Before going to sleep that night, I had been looking at an
> illustrated Bible that had been given to me by Fay. In it there
> was a picture of the Crucifixion and I had been reading about
> the Crucifixion.[15]

According to the psychiatric report on Cloretta Robinson, the young black Baptist girl from California:

> Significant past events consisted of her reading a religious book about the Crucifixion, *Crossroads,* by John Webster, approximately one week prior to bleeding and about a month before Easter; the book was deeply religious with strong emotional overtones. Four days prior to the bleeding she watched a television movie on the Crucifixion that very much involved her emotionally, causing a vivid dream about it that night.[16]

In respect of Jane Hunt and her visions of the Virgin Mary and the infant Jesus, she told me on my visit to her that when she was a child:

> In my bedroom there was [a view towards] a stained glass window. It used to be the chapel [in the Derbyshire village of Ripley] that was facing my bedroom window when I was small. And I used to be able to see through those stained glass windows . . . and I could see . . . he was in a cradle with Mary rocking him. And all the cows and the sheep, everything was in this stained glass window . . . Jesus was in there, and I could see him every night before I went to sleep.[17]

It seems that the stigmatic temperament is highly susceptible to empathy with distress, illness or suffering. There may even be an argument that the whole sudden onset of stigmatisations in the thirteenth century was due to the new, realistic fashion in artistic portrayals of Jesus that came into being shortly before St Francis of Assisi's time.

In previous centuries Christian churches throughout Europe had been decorated according to the stiff and formal Byzantine style. Even when Jesus was portrayed on the cross with the lance in his side, he was represented in a long garment and with his eyes wide open. To show suffering, extreme emotion, or more than a token amount of blood, was unthinkable. Around the second half of the twelfth century changes began to creep in. The taking down of Jesus's body from the cross was shown much more realistically. His eyes were now portrayed closed in death, and the hold women and his disciples as clearly riven with grief.[18] Crucifixes became more bloody, Jesus's body more obviously tortured. It may have seemed little more than a change of fashion, but it encouraged an empathy with Jesus and would have provided a powerful charge to anyone emotionally wrapped in the contemplation of his sufferings. So could this have been what prompted the sudden flush of stigmatics within little more than a generation?

This might seem reasonable enough, but it falls far short of a full explanation. However vivid the paintings or stories, if all is mere illusion, why such extraordinary behaviour? And why should it so dramatically affect the flesh of their bodies? Why such extremes? There has to be some other factor involved.

AN INTRIGUING LINK

IF a common factor among stigmatics is protracted contemplation of the sufferings of Christ, equally evident is the preliminary of some extreme form of physical or mental stress. What seems to have changed St Francis was the shock of imprisonment followed by illness. His fasts and mortifications added to the physical stresses so that he was probably near breaking point at the time of the onset of his stigmata.

In the case of St Maria Maddalena de' Pazzi, although she had a comfortable enough childhood, her most striking peculiarity was a penchant for torturing herself. Catharine Emmerich had an upbringing of grinding poverty, followed, on at last becoming a nun, by the terrors of being caught up in political suppression of the convents. She knew for real the pains of destitution and near-starvation.

If we next turn to Domenica Lazzari, at the age of eighteen she suffered a night of abject terror alone in a mill, thereupon taking to her bed, which in turn led to her stigmata. Louise Lateau was at the age of eleven gored by a bull. This was followed by serious illness. Teresa Higginson suffered at the age of five her family's over-dramatised grief at the death of her younger brother. Then came a variety of falls (one into a sawpit), for which she had to spend long spells in bed. Like St Maria Maddalena de' Pazzi, she indulged in excessive mortifications, creating for her bedding an old piece of sacking bristling with knitting needles and sharp sticks, and applying red-hot coals to her breasts.

Therese Neumann sustained a serious injury while fighting the fire at the inn, then lapsed into paralyses and blindness. Bertha Mrazek's physical state on being brought into the shrine at Halle has already been fully described, as has that of Dorothy Kerin. Even Padre Pio, early on in his monkish vocation, became wasted through excessive fasting, and like Dorothy Kerin, was diagnosed as suffering from tuberculosis.

Jane Hunt suffered a series of traumas. During her childhood she had been deaf, partly as a result of which she spent long spells day-dreaming in her room, or in an under-the-table refuge she felt to be her 'church'. On marrying, she suffered two particularly tragic miscarriages. In one she herself nearly died; in the other a seven month old boy foetus strangled on the umbilical cord as she unwittingly gave birth to him on the toilet.

In several of the cases cited above the physical illnesses could have been what psychiatrists term 'hysterical' – that is, brought about by the mental state of the patient rather than by a physical cause. With regard to Therese Neumann, after her fire-fighting accident a compensation claim was filed with the Insurance Company of the Upper Palatinate on the grounds that the accident, sustained while working for her employer, had robbed her of the capacity for any further such employment. The resultant medical investigation reported in 1919, seven years before her stigmatisation, that she had 'no appreciable lesion' that could account for her paralyses, and that the cause was 'a very grave traumatic hysteria'.[1]

A similar diagnosis could be applied to Bertha Mrazek's condition prior to her 'cure' at Halle, to the demon-possessed Soeur Jeanne des Anges, and to the bed-ridden states of several other stigmatics.

Given that hysteria can be as communicable to others as any biological infection, it is easy to understand how in the thirteenth century the Dominican convent of Adelshausen at Freiburg-im-Breisgau produced no less than six stigmatics – Grunberg of Kastelberg, Luggi Löscherin, Agnes of Nordera, Adelaide of Brisach, Güte Tuschelin and Gertrude Küchlin – all within a few years of each other.

But simply diagnosing stigmatics as hysterical, however justifiable, does little more than attach another label to them. We still need to understand what is happening. This leads in turn to the question of whether there is any recognised psychiatric condition in which similar features can be observed. Indeed there is, in the form of a rare and puzzling phenomenon known as multiple personality. This was popularised a generation ago by the case of 'Eve' of the best-selling book and block-busting film *The Three Faces of Eve*.[2]

At first sight multiple personality seems unrelated to stigmatisation. Its primary feature is of the sufferer suddenly 'splitting' into a personality quite different from his or her normal self. In the Eve case, the subject was ostensibly a simple, neat and conservative Georgia housewife. But at unexpected moments she would suddenly snap into a personality who called herself Chris Costner, and who would speak coarsely and wear provocative dresses. Eve, whose real-life name is Chris Sizemore, has since described in her autobiography,[3] how over some twenty years she found herself the prey to some twenty invading personalities of this kind who would take her over in such a way that she would be amnesic during those times they took charge. Her 'normal' self would, for instance, find in her wardrobe the dresses she had purchased while she was 'Chris Costner' and be consumed by embarrassment and confusion – not to mention finding herself financially out of pocket. There might be days, even weeks, for which all memory was completely, lost. Different personalities even had different handwriting.

Such is the hold of the condition that in the case of another sufferer, Billy Milligan from Ohio,[4] the personalities that took him over drove him into serious crime. One called Arthur would plan robberies and rapes, which would then be put into action by a second, sadistic personality called Ragen who spoke with a heavy Slavic accent. Incongruously, a third lesbian personality called Adalena would carry out the rape itself. It was quite common for the personalities inhabiting Eve, Billy Milligan and others not only to speak with different voices and to have different tastes and habits, but also to be of a different sex or age from the 'parent' body, even talking and behaving like children. One of Eve's personalities was an apparently five year old 'Banana Split Girl', so wilful that she would eat only banana splits. Billy Milligan's young man's body was also home to a three year old girl personality called Christene, whose passion was drawing and painting butterflies.

One of the first signs that this strange condition has a link with stigmatics is the common background of severe stress. When Eve was only two she was on the scene as the corpse of a drunk was hauled from an irrigation ditch where previously she had been told a monster lurked. Not long afterwards she witnessed

St Francis of Assisi, the first known stigmatic.

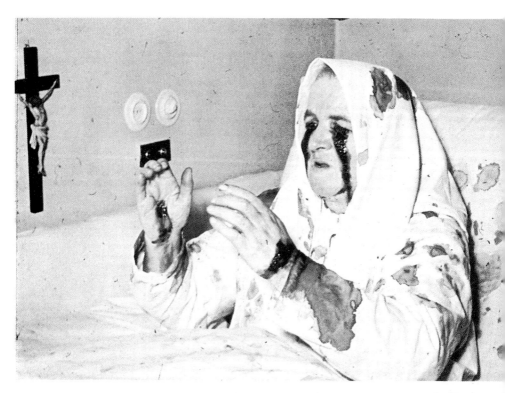

Therese Neumann during her reliving of a Good Friday passion (above), and showing 'nailwounds' in the backs of her hands (right).

Padre Pio in his later years, celebrating Mass.

The Crucifix before which Padre Pio was praying when stigmatised.

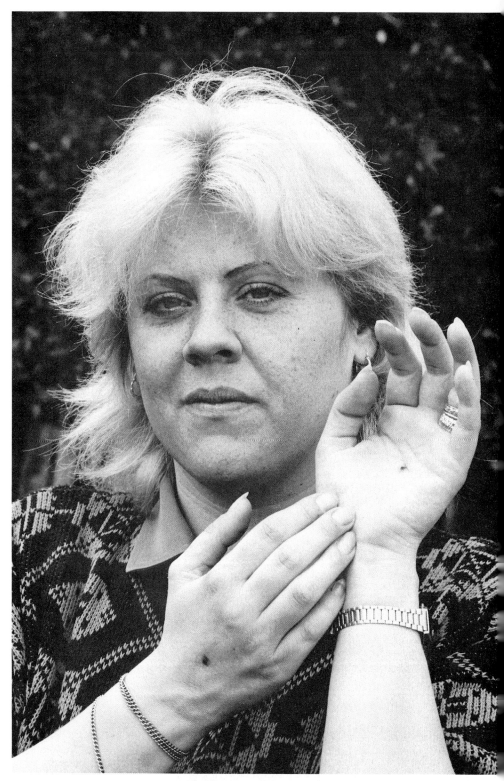

Living English stigmatic Jane Hunt.

Stigmatic Spanish Archbishop Clemente Dominguez bleeding from his side-wound while experiencing a vision of Jesus' passion (above), and the 'Crown of thorns' wounds on Clemente Dominguez's forehead (below).

St Teresa of Avila in visionary trance.

Jesus stretched and crucified on the cross, from the Holkham Bible. It seems no coincidence that stigmata followed the proliferation of a greater realism and gruesomeness in representations of Christ's passion and crucifixion.

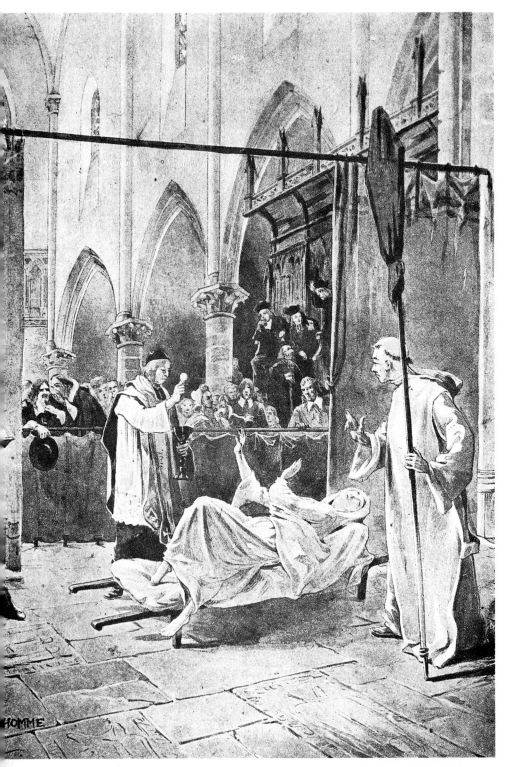

Soeur Jeanne des Anges of Loudun, who was reported to have manifested a similar bloody cross on her forehead during the seventeenth century.

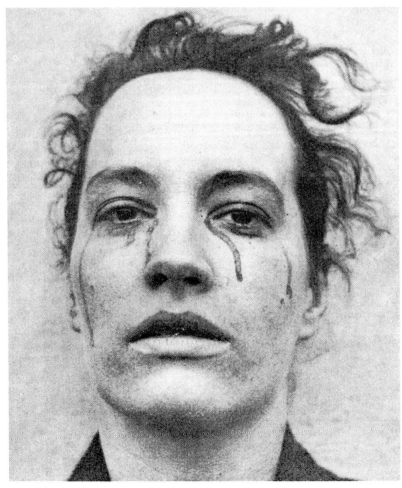

Elizabeth K, bleeding from her eyes, as hypnotically induced by Dr Alfred Lechler.

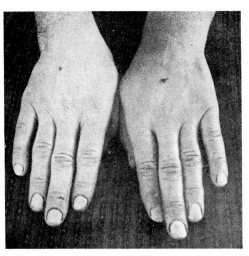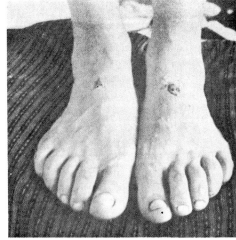

Elizabeth K's hand and foot 'nail' wounds.

a sawmill accident in which a man was literally cut in two. Billy Milligan as a child suffered terribly at the hands of a step-father who locked him in cupboards, shut him in boxes, and subjected him to merciless thrashings and attacks of a sexual nature, including anal intercourse.

Another multiple personality sufferer, 'Sybil',[5] was similarly abused by a schizophrenic mother who would stuff a towel down her throat to stop her crying, then suspend her, legs forced apart, from the light cord, or fill her vagina with cold water and tie her to a piano leg while she pounded out Bach, Beethoven and Chopin.

The case for a link increases when we find that many of the ailments suffered by multiple personality patients are reminiscent of those we have come across in stigmatics. For instance, two of Eve's personalities, one a child and one an adult, affected blindness, just as Therese Neumann and Bertha Mrazek had done. Eve, Billy Milligan and Sybil all suffered from twitches reminiscent of stigmatics' convulsions.

There also emerge from the multiple personality cases signs of near-stigmatic phenomena. While in her Chris Costner personality, Eve would develop an angry urticaria rash from wearing nylon stockings, but had no such reaction when her normal self was in control. She has described in her autobiography how one evening shortly before her fiftieth birthday she involuntarily 'flipped' back to relive a childhood accident in which her clothes had been set alight by the fire heating the family washtub. In a shrill voice typical of a three year old she began calling out: 'Mummy, I'm burning! Mummy, I'm burning!', at the same time rolling on the floor and tearing at her dress. To the astonishment of those who rushed to help her, the skin of her right arm and shoulder had turned a livid red colour, and an old puckered scar from the original injury became dramatically reinflamed. When a wet towel was applied to her arm it literally steamed from the heat.[6] This invokes new credibility to the hot blood and water said to have poured from the sides of Francesca de Serrone and Angela della Pace.

The interesting question is thus: if multiple personality sufferers exhibit symptoms akin to stigmatics, do stigmatics likewise exhibit symptoms akin to multiple personality sufferers? A review of the case histories indicates an affirmative answer.

A case in point is that of Anna Maria Castreca,[7] who was born at Fabriano, Italy, in 1670. She was taught to read at the age of three by an uncle of whom she was terrified. When Anna Maria was only eight she lost both her parents, and was sent to be educated at a Benedictine convent where the nuns included two aunts of whom she was also terrified. She now appears to have experienced some form of vision, after which, although she had previously been gifted in reading, she was found to have lost all memory of everything she had ever learnt about reading and sewing and had to learn these skills all over again.

Although the original memories came back to her after a year just as suddenly as they had disappeared, she was now prey to further psychological disorders. Around 1690, when she was twenty, she suffered a long illness during which she lost all external feeling – a typical multiple personality occurrence. On looking at herself in a mirror in a pretty hat, she would see instead the image of Jesus crowned with thorns and dripping with blood, urging her to become one of the female branch of Franciscans – another occurrence for which parallels can be found among multiple personality cases. When at the age of twenty-six Anna Maria joined the austere Capuchins at Fabriano, these problems became worse. She found herself seemingly taken over by evil entities that would throw her into contortions and cause her to swear and curse when she wanted to pray. As in the cases of Eve, Sybil and Billy Milligan, she would take on the personality of a child. As described by her biographer Buti, on such occasions:

> she ceased to be her natural self, and whatever was said or done she paid no heed to anything, but prattled away with a most charming grace of manner, seeming in look, in language, and in all she did, to be just a little child of five years old.[8]

She also suffered from spells in which one part of her appeared not to know what the other was doing. On several occasions she was found in the middle of the night with the keys of the convent in her hands, about to leave. Anna Maria might have passed every diagnostic test as a case of multiple personality, except that in addition to all her other symptoms she happens to have received stigmata.

Therese Neumann and other stigmatics also displayed similar behaviour. Quite unaware of the psychological implications, one after another of Therese Neumann's biographers has described how she would lapse into certain distinctive states of mind, one of these quite specifically with the personality of a five year old child. According to Friedrich von Lama's observations of this state:

> She does not even grasp the sense of words like brother, sister, parents, etc . . . and does not understand the meaning of figures either. Describing the uncovering of the cross, she tells us that our Lord's cross (the longer beam of which was in fact divided into two parts) was made up of four pieces: 'There was one, and one, and one, and one.' 'So there were four?' asked Fr Naber. 'Four? I don't know. There was one, and one, and one, and one.' 'That of the good thief had three.' 'Three? I don't know. One, and one, and one!'[9]

Another of Therese's mental states was described by her biographers as 'elevated calm', during which she spoke of herself in the third person. Typical of this were her predictions of her next bleeding or vision. For instance: 'She will have a vision this evening at eight'. This is reminiscent of Eve's secondary personality's reply to psychiatrist Thigpen's questioning of why she used the name Chris Costner: 'Because Eve White is her, not me.'[10] On another occasion Therese Neumann is reported to have replied to parish priest Father Naber with the words: 'You can't speak to Therese now, she is asleep.'[11] In this instance she not only used the third person, but also, in the original German, the familiar form 'du' for 'you' – a lack of respect quite untypical of the normal Therese, and again indicative of a shift in personality.

If for 'multiple personality' we substitute the older term 'possession', then it is evident that stigmatic after stigmatic has experienced this in some form or another. Sixteenth century stigmatic Domenica of Paradise certainly believed herself to be beset by devils, as did St Maria Maddalena de' Pazzi. In the seventeenth century Soeur Jeanne des Anges of Loudun is known to have been spectacularly 'possessed' before she received her forehead cross and the names on her hand. In the same century the Italian Dominican nun Angela Della Pace purported to suffer likewise, as did French Carmelite Marguerite Parigot, subsequently Marguerite of the Blessed Sacrament, whose diabolic attacks were so devastating that doctors cauterised and even trepanned her skull. In the nineteenth century there was no let-up. Teresa Higginson shocked her lodgings companions in Ariel Street, Bootle, by the violence of her apparent 'possessions'. These were described at first hand by one of those companions, Elizabeth Roberts:

I was falling asleep when a loud shaking of the window near
my bed awakened me. The night was calm. I was disturbed
by a loud noise as of someone being slapped on the face. Then
followed loud knocks as of someone being shaken and banged
about the room, then Miss Higginson's room door was shaken
very violently and terrible, unearthly screams were heard . . .[12]

If it might be thought that genial and well-balanced Padre Pio
was free of anything of this kind, nothing could be further from
the truth. While training for his vocation he too was reportedly
assailed by evil spirits, sometimes visiting him in the guise of
his friary companions, sometimes taking him over in such a way
that his cell would subsequently be found in total disarray, with
books torn, blankets strewn over the floor, and ink spattered on
the walls.[13]

It would take a whole book to explore all the parallels, case
by case. But what is evident is that stigmata and multiple personality seem to be so closely linked that they could be two different
aspects of the same phenomenon. Both seem to be stress-induced,
seemingly as a response to a metabolism tortured to the end of
its tether. In both we find the individual caught up in a flight
from reality, on the one hand into a fantasy personality providing
some form of release or escape from the constraints on the every-
day self, and on the other into an established fantasy world of
religious figures and a personal dramatisation of the events surrounding the death of Jesus.

But however much the mental state may be a fantasy one, its
physical accompaniments seem to be generated at so profound
a level that they look extraordinarily convincing even when all
reason tells us not to be deceived. Thus when psychiatrist Thigpen
first saw Eve's change of personality, what shook him to his pro-
fessional roots was the facial switch that occurred before his very
eyes. The previously demure and tightly constrained woman
assumed first a look of eerie blankness, then a quite new, mischie-
vous and sexually provocative expression that, as he was soon
to learn, was the coming out of secondary personality Chris
Costner. Similarly, when observing Therese Neumann, of the pro-
foundest effect on her biographer Anni Spiegl was the witnessing
of Therese's almost palpably real emotions when caught up in
her visions:

Anyone who had the opportunity of watching Therese's facial
expression during her visions can no longer have any doubts

as to their authenticity. Joy, fear, amazement, inquisitiveness and horror passed over her face in turn within a matter of seconds. . . .[14]

And hysterical though they might be labelled, there can be no doubting that the blindnesses and paralyses that have affected stigmatics and multiple personality cases have been in their own way real enough for those affected by them, and those trying to treat them. Equally genuine has been another feature not yet mentioned, the facility to at least partly anaesthetise localised areas of the body. In the case of St Francis of Assisi this had a very real application when, as a result of the eye ailment he had contracted in Egypt, a medieval physician decided that the only remedy lay in cauterisation – searing with a red-hot iron. According to St Francis's faithful Brother Leo:

> On a certain day the physician came to him, who, considering the disease, said to Blessed Francis that he would make a cautery over the jaw up to the eyebrow of that eye which was weaker than the other. And having placed the iron in the fire to make the cautery, Blessed Francis . . . spoke thus to the fire, 'My brother fire, noble and useful among all other creatures, be kindly to me in this hour – but I pray our Creator . . . will so temper thy heat that I may be able to sustain it.' We who were with him then did flee, out of pity and compassion for him, and the physician alone remained with him, but when the cautery was made we returned to him, who said to us: 'Oh cowards and of little faith, why did you fly? In truth I say unto you, that I have felt no pain nor the heat of the fire.' And the physician marvelled greatly, for all the veins from the ear to the eyebrow had to be cut open.[15]

If this sounds a little too like medieval make-believe, we need to be reminded that Anna Maria Castreca was reported to have manifested a similar desensitisation of her body. And when in October 1925 Padre Pio had to be operated on for a hernia, he refused the customary chloroform anaesthetic, and endured the two-hour operation with a fortitude that astonished his doctors, repeating the performance for the removal of a large cyst two years later.[16]

Again we are bound to ask, how is all this to be understood? And again, without being able to give a direct answer, there is a significant observation that comes to mind. If we ask what has been the single most successful method of treating multiple personality cases, there is but one answer: hypnosis. Although still only dimly understood, it was by putting Eve, Sybil, Billy Milligan and others into a hypnotic trance that their respective psychiatrists were able to unlock each internal zoo of hidden personalities, talk them through the traumas and eventually restore them to normality.

Similarly, recalling the auto-anaesthesia of St Francis and Padre Pio, if we ask by what non-physical technique such desensitisation may be effected, we find the same answer: hypnosis. If we consider the state of mind in which stigmatics receive their visions, their closest resemblance is to a hypnotic trance. There also seems to have been something hypnotic in the way certain of the stigmatics' confessors were able to instruct wounds to open and close, as in the case of seventeenth century stigmatic St Veronica Giuliani. According to her own account:

> Sometimes he (the confessor) said to me: 'I do not wish it [her side-wound] to close before such a day or such an hour.' And in fact it would happen so. . . . If I am not mistaken the Bishop on one occasion did the same thing. He came here with certain of God's servants and they wished to see this wound in the side open, to my great sorrow. Then the Bishop told me that he would come again the next day but wished the wound to be closed. And so precisely it came about.[17]

Furthermore, if, we think back to the curiously consistent chronology of certain stigmatics' wounds, there is again one familiar phenomenon to which these are akin: post-hypnotic suggestion, the method of 'programming' hypnotised subjects to carry out certain tasks, in response to chronological or other cues, months or even years after having been woken from the original trance.

So we come to what is perhaps the most crucial question of all. If stigmatic and multiple personality mental states resemble a hypnotic trance, could it be that under controlled conditions a skilled hypnotist might be able to induce stigmata phenomena? If this were possible, it would constitute the greatest proof that whatever the nature of the underlying mechanism, stigmatics really have quite spontaneously produced the sort of wounds claimed of them over the centuries. But is it possible? That is the question we must next to try to answer.

STIGMATA REPLICATED

ONE of the popular suppositions about hypnosis is that if a subject is told he or she is about to have a cigarette stubbed out on their hand, and the hand is touched with nothing more harmful than a pencil, the skin will react as if it had genuinely been burnt, and produce a blister.

The reality is by no means so straightforward. Undoubtedly, deep trance subjects respond in all sorts of bizarre ways to the suggestions of a skilled hypnotist – adopting cataleptic rigidity, becoming insensitive to pinpricks, or counting as if the number nine does not exist, to name but a few. Furthermore, if the 'lighted cigarette' suggestion is made to them, they may well flinch as if burnt, even though touched with something quite harmless. But as demonstrated in controlled experiments, normally they will not blister.[1]

However, there are rare but significant exceptions to this rule. These, fascinatingly, turn out to be of the hysteric/highly stressed type common among stigmatics and multiple personality sufferers. According to a study by psychologist Gordon Paul[2] of the University of Illinois, those who have genuinely exhibited the blister reaction have included a victim of shell shock, a student who had a sleep-walking problem, a man who had suffered hysterical blindness as a result of wartime experiences, several women specifically labelled hysterics, and, not least, sufferers from a peculiar skin condition known as dermographia.

Some background history of stress, yet again seems to be a powerful contributor to this particular variety of flesh change.

But before being totally satisfied that this is the case we need first to know something more about the condition called dermographia.

Dermographia was first recognised by the great school of French psychologists who worked at the Salpetrière in Paris at the end of the last century. Its key feature is skin so sensitive that if a pattern is traced upon it with even the bluntest of instruments this will develop into a fully raised pattern visible even at a distance. This reaction, often spectacular, is apparently little different from that which everyone suffers when stung by nettles, except that the dermographia patient experiences no itching and, exhibits the lividity precisely according to whatever pattern has been traced.

We may now be able to understand better how certain stigmatics produce lettering on their skin – for instance, how Soeur Jeanne des Anges managed to exhibit names on her left hand, and how Breton peasant girl Marie-Julie Jahenny manifested the 'O crux ave' and other features on her breast. In such cases, while the skin reaction may have been genuine enough, arguably the lettering was produced, consciously or otherwise, by the individual tracing the outline with a finger, hence for instance the choice of the left hand as writing base on the part of the right-handed Soeur Jeanne.

What is also apparent in these instances is that the history of stress still remains an important factor. A medical dictionary definition for the type of person likely to exhibit dermographia states:

> The sufferers are sometimes hysterical women, sometimes chronic alcoholics, sometimes epileptics or victims of other disorders of the nervous system.[3]

This begs the question: what happens when a hysteric or highly stressed individual is given the hypnotic suggestion that he or she is suffering from some wound. Will anything resembling stigmata appear?

The first indications that something of this kind is possible derive from some rare instances among those exhibiting past lives under hypnosis. These have seemed to manifest wounds consistent with injuries supposedly inflicted during an earlier incarnation. For instance, one subject of Liverpool hypnotherapist Joe Keeton, Ann Dowling, in ordinary life a pleasant housewife from Huyton, under hypnosis became Sarah Williams, purportedly a wretchedly poor orphan girl living in the slums of Liverpool in the first half of the nineteenth century.[4] As relived by Ann, Sarah seemed to meet a violent end by being beaten to death by an Irish navvy. Every morning after Keeton caused her to hypnotically relive Sarah's death, the real-life Ann woke with bruises consistent with the punishment meted out on the hallucinated Sarah.[5]

A similar reaction has been reported of another of Keeton's subjects, Pauline McKay of Ellesmere Port, who hypnotically recalled a past life as Kitty Jay, a Devon woman who reputedly committed suicide by hanging herself. According to those who witnessed Pauline reliving this event, her neck was seen to flare up with a livid red rope-mark just at the moment of her re-enacting Kitty's fatal drop.[6]

Interesting as these examples are, for us the crucial question is whether, under controlled conditions, anyone has been hypnotically persuaded to produce specific crucifixion wounds. For the key case we must look back to the Germany of 1928 – when interest surrounding Therese Neumann was at its height – and to the consulting room of psychiatrist Dr Alfred Lechler, into which was ushered a seriously disturbed twenty-six year old patient who, for purposes of medical anonymity, has become referred to as Elizabeth K.

Lechler's little-known report[7] on Elizabeth shows that her background was that of a classic multiple personality case. Of peasant parentage, but intelligent and sensitive, she was only six when her mother died. Shortly afterwards she came under the wing of a tyrannical step-mother who seems to have done her best to make her home life an unhappy one.

At school Elizabeth's lively imagination ensured that she was top of the class for literary composition, but when she was fifteen she caught the influenza that decimated Europe after the First World War. She survived, but thereafter began to suffer involuntary tremblings of her head, right arm and leg, and cramps in her joints.

Hypnotic treatment was available, and with this, and an opportunity to work away from home, Elizabeth's problems temporarily cleared, only to recur as soon as her step-mother demanded that she return home to help with domestic duties. There followed headaches, nausea and double vision, then a four-day bout of unconsciousness, followed by paralysis to her right side and loss of all feeling in some parts of her body.

So acute did these problems become that, hysteria or otherwise, Elizabeth found herself unable to sit, move her head, or speak.

Her mouth became so distorted that she could eat only with great difficulty, and she suffered disorders with her bladder and bowels. On the suspicion of a brain tumour she underwent brain surgery, but to little avail, and as in the case of Therese Neumann her prolonged stays in bed brought on severe bedsores. Neither electrical nor hypnotic treatment brought her much relief, and suicidal urges seem to have been close to the surface. On one occasion she swallowed two sewing needles, and on another she fell downstairs. She refused food and had to be force-fed.

Then, a few months after she had been referred to Dr Lechler, he decided, because she was conscientious and hard working, to ask her to work as a domestic servant in his own household. One advantage was that he could keep a careful eye on her, and from this point on, aided by Lechler's periodic use of hypnotherapy, Elizabeth's health seemed markedly to improve, despite a tendency to take upon herself any medical symptoms she happened to hear about. For instance, one day after a conversation about a hernia case, a fall prompted her to assume all the symptoms associated with a hernia, even though she was quite unharmed. There was also an occasion when she was supposed to make a duty call to her family home, but began coughing blood as if she had contracted tuberculosis, even though, as tests proved, her lungs were perfectly clear.

Then came Good Friday, 1932. On that day Elizabeth attended a talk on the Crucifixion, illustrated with slides showing the various stages of Jesus's sufferings. In the course of this she apparently felt she was experiencing in her hands and feet the pains of the nails being driven in, and complained of this when she returned to the Lechler household that evening.

It was this which gave Lechler an idea. Knowing of the Therese Neumann case, and suspecting that Elizabeth's pains might be indications of a similar disposition, he decided to try to develop stigmata in Elizabeth by hypnotic suggestion. Having induced hypnosis, instead of suggesting to her that the pains in her hands and feet would go away, he directed her to focus her mind on the idea of real nails being driven into her hands and feet.

Like many hypnotic subjects, when brought out of her trance Elizabeth had no memory of what she had been told. But her condition the next morning, Easter Saturday, told its own story. The centres of her palms and feet were riven with red and swollen marks the size of a penny, with the skin around them torn and weeping. She was in great distress, believing herself to have become another Therese Neumann, but at a total loss to understand how or why this should be happening to her.

Lechler calmed her down, explaining how the marks had come about, and said that he should be able to make them vanish in the same way that they had appeared. But first he said he hoped she might help him by co-operating in certain experiments so that he could better understand what was happening.

On gaining her agreement, he asked her to try, during ordinary waking consciousness, to visualise the lurid tears of blood she had seen in press photographs of Therese Neumann. While she did the housework she was to keep thinking about these images, and to try to feel them as if they were happening to her own person.

Elizabeth co-operated, and within hours she presented herself to Lechler in a pitiful state. Blood was welling up from inside her eyelids and pouring down her cheeks, a sight so extraordinary that Lechler immediately photographed her. Alarmed and astonished, he suggested that the bloody tears should immediately cease flowing, which they did while he watched. He followed up with instructions for the healing of the nail wounds, which disappeared in the course of the next two days.

To Lechler it was vindication that the key to stigmata lay in psychology, not theology, and he went on to repeat the experiment with Elizabeth in a variety of ways. As one variant, while she was hypnotised he suggested that a crown of thorns was being placed on her head. Although he merely brushed her forehead with his fingers, she immediately jerked in severe pain, and the next morning showed him her forehead covered with irregularly-shaped puncture-type wounds which, on his suggestion, oozed blood within an hour.

As another variant Lechler suggested to Elizabeth that she was Jesus carrying the cross. Although, because this suggestion was given under hypnosis, she had no conscious memory of it when awake, the next day she complained of severe pains in her left shoulder. She held her left arm awkwardly and moved with a leftward lean, and when her shoulder was examined it was found to be red and swollen. On the appropriate suggestion the injuries and the pain disappeared. This happened far more quickly than would have been the case with real injuries of the same kind.

Like the doctors who fifty years previously had tested Louise Lateau, Lechler wanted to rule out beyond question the possibility that Elizabeth had somehow inflicted the wounds upon herself.

He accordingly tried to create circumstances in which he could see these for himself as they manifested. At first he had some difficulty, for Elizabeth seemed to go through a phase in which, although she appeared to feel pains when these were suggested to her, she manifested virtually no physical change. Lechler came to attribute this to improved mental well-being on her part, again suggesting the crucial role of stress in the onset of stigmata.

But then in August 1932, Lechler sensed that Elizabeth was once more likely to be responsive, and having arranged for round-the-clock observation, repeated his hypnotic suggestions, this time with particular emphasis on her feeling crucifixion nails being driven into her hands and feet. According to his report:

After a few hours under constant observation an area the size of a five mark piece appeared, a bluey coloured swelling on the top of the feet, and in the middle were several pea-sized bright red spots. Elizabeth groaned frequently due to immense pain. On the soles of the feet they were only small red spots. Due to fatigue Elizabeth fell asleep several times and each time the redness faded. This went on until the evening and through the night. When Elizabeth was not concentrating the pain went. And so it would increase and decrease as the suggestions were put to her. At 9 am under personal observation blood the size of a pinhead emerged from the spot at the top of the left foot. Immediately after that the red area on the sole of the left foot opened and there also a drop of blood emerged. After a few minutes the right foot followed in the same manner. Then it was suggested that the scars on the hands should open and blood should emerge, which did happen as I personally observed. When Elizabeth stopped concentrating on the bleeding it soon stopped. The next morning it was suggested again that the scars which had closed up again should open and start to bleed. After half an hour the scars opened and a bloodless watery liquid emerged.

All the mentioned experiments were carried out under strict control of myself and reliable nurses, and the results during that period never varied. I myself was present when the blood on the hands and feet emerged. A few days later it was suggested to Elizabeth that a crown of thorns was put on her head and after an hour several red marks the size of a pea appeared on her forehead. In the middle of these marks red blood spots the size of pinheads appeared. During the following hours the blood spots increased and from several of them blood emerged. Some drops were large enough to roll down the forehead. During all that time Elizabeth complained of headache and a sensation of pinpricks. The continuous observation of the proceedings was done by me and the already mentioned nurses. I myself could clearly see the emergence of the blood in several places.

A week later it was again suggested to Elizabeth that she should shed blood-stained tears. After an hour her eyelids and cheeks started to get red and she complained of stinging in the eyes. After three hours her lower eyelids began to show blood spots which gradually spread. The lids started to swell. After seven hours blood emerged from the inner corners of the eyes. Next morning, after several hours of concentration and under constant observation, blood emerged in greater amounts, especially from the inner corners of the eye. It ran over the edge of the lids and the lower lids were soon covered in congealed blood . . .[8]

The significance of all this is profound. Effectively Lechler can be said to have established more authoritatively than anyone before or since that spontaneous bleedings of the type attributed to stigmatics during the last seven centuries really do happen, and that these can be demonstrated under properly controlled conditions. He can also be said to have established that a fundamental key to the phenomenon is hypnosis, and that the stigmatic, even without having been formally hypnotised, seems to be, during his or her bleedings, in a mental and physical state effectively indistinguishable from hypnosis.

Particularly significant was an experiment which Lechler conducted in May 1932, in which he gave Elizabeth a copy of the Bible and asked her to read carefully through the gospel of St John, studying the accompanying pictures and thinking herself into the New Testament scene. Lechler described Elizabeth's reaction:

After fifteen minutes she slowly closed her eyes, put the Bible aside, took deep breaths and groaned frequently while I watched her. I asked her: 'Do you see anything?' She didn't answer. Soon her groaning became louder. She opened her eyes for a time and cried. After asking her again whether she saw anything she answered with several pauses: 'They want to crucify our Saviour . . . crucify him, crucify him. Pilate cannot find him guilty. Jesus is quite calm. They are putting the red cloak on him.'

She was crying loudly now. 'One is particularly angry . . . he is hitting him in the face. Our Saviour is carrying a cross . . . the cross himself . . . three crosses . . .'

Suddenly she stretched out her arms and got into the position of a crucified person. Her breathing nearly stopped, and she said quietly: 'Now it is finished.'

I asked her what was happening. She did not answer for several minutes. At last, after demanding to be answered, her breathing became normal again and she replied between sobs: 'I have seen the Saviour on the cross. And then I was hanged there myself. There were the thieves hanging. I am a sinner and I belong to the thieves. Our Saviour was on the cross beside me. And then I didn't see any more.'[9]

Despite the obvious source of inspiration, and the contrivance of hypnosis, no-one reading such an account can fail to be struck by the way all the characteristic stigmatic features are there – the scene unfolding before the eyes and being described in the present tense; the intense emotional reactions, complete with weeping and groaning; and the complete involvement with the scene, to the extent, unprompted by Lechler, of Elizabeth seeing herself as one of the two thieves crucified with Jesus. And all this alongside her production of crucifixion wounds.

Lechler went on:

During the time following these events I hypnotised her several times suggesting to her to concentrate on the suffering of Jesus, but to imagine herself being among the crowd and not on the cross. The results were always the same. After being put under hypnosis she soon 'saw' the events taking place and her facial expression and movements of the body told of the inner turmoil she was going through. Even when suggesting some other event to her she would soon see herself in that role and her face would take on a different expression. Especially touching was the experience of her being a child and Jesus as the friend of the children. Her face took on a childish expression, she would wave exuberantly with both arms and speak in a childish voice, and make caressing movements.[10]

We can also note in this Elizabeth's behaviour as a child, just as we have seen earlier in the cases of multiple personality Eve and stigmatics Anna Maria Castreca and Therese Neumann. She even apparently spoke of herself, multiple-personality style, in the third person. When undergoing electric shock treatment before becoming Lechler's patient, she reportedly remarked: 'Miss K. will walk properly all by herself without being electrified by you.' and 'Miss K. will be happy again as soon as she won't have to do such heavy work any more.'

Now we can see that there was nothing haphazard or accidental about the power of the sources we suspected had their influence on other stigmatics past and present: all the meditations on the more lurid aspects of Jesus's Passion on the part of St Francis of Assisi and numerous others in religious vocations; the Veronica painting and other holy pictures that dominated the living room of Polish-born Australian Mrs H.; the bloody crucifix before which Padre Pio worshipped; the illustrated Bible given to Ethel Chapman by radio evangelist Fay Roberts; the *Crossroads* book read by Californian Baptist girl Cloretta Robinson. All these, arguably played their part in the chemistry leading to the specific reaction of stigmata, and we now at least dimly discern some of the dynamics involved.

The key feature in this is that, given such dynamics, the flesh can and does change according to visual or verbal inputs. A change in form can be willed upon the flesh by something beyond the normal consciousness of the stigmatic, without there being any justification for regarding that something as divine. Indeed, the fact that stigmatics exhibit wounds in the semblance of those specifically of Jesus seems simply to be because so many have so intensely identified with the sufferings of this particular individual. Although proper sources are lacking, there are said to have been Moslems who have produced on their bodies wounds associated with their prophet Mohammed.

If we need further evidence of non-stigmatic wounds, we need only look to certain cases of so-called abreaction attested in medical literature. One such, reported in 1946 by British psychiatrist Dr Robert Moody,[11] concerned an emotionally disturbed army officer who needed treatment because of an alarming tendency to sleep-walk. Years before, while serving in India, the officer had had to be tied up with ropes because of this problem. While under Moody's care he would sleep-walk around the hospital grounds. Although he returned safely, for Moody the astonishing feature was that on his skin there developed weals and indentations exactly corresponding to the marks that would have been left by the ropes when he had been tied years before. Moody photographed these and even observed bleeding from them.

Similarly, a woman patient of Moody's manifested on her body marks in the exact shape of an unusually-carved stick with which her father had beaten her when she had been a child.[12] The lesson of such examples is that, given a suitably stressed individual, any meaningful mental input can be translated into an extreme physical reaction.

If all this thinking is valid, then the implications are truly extraordinary. What is important is not so much the finding that stigmata are not miraculous marks of divine favour. Indeed this news would be of no surprise even to the Roman Catholic Church, which, as evident from its scepticism towards Padre Pio and others, has clearly suspected as much for a very long time.

Rather, the truly significant feature is that the flesh really does change, in an extraordinarily dramatic way, in response to mental activity, and that the power of mind over matter is phenomenally more powerful than previously thought possible – though it appears that individuals have to be in a highly stressed state for this process to happen.

A first reaction to this might be: well, so what? What use is it to anyone to be able to produce wounds at will, when all medical endeavour is directed to the very reverse? But this is to miss the point. If the mind really can spontaneously produce wounds in this way, can it also be persuaded to do the reverse? Can it stem the uncheckable bleeding of a haemophiliac, or shrink a malignant tumour? As we are about to discover, there are some remarkable pointers that this might genuinely be possible.

⇌ 10 ⇌

POWER WITHIN?

IN all that we have seen so far, some strange but physically unin-
jured individuals have, by some power whose workings we have
yet to fully understand, quite needlessly produced on their bodies
serious wounds. While these individuals have often yearned to
share something of the experiences of Jesus, no-one in their right
mind would want to be disfigured in such a way. Yet this has
happened, and happened, so far as we can judge, through some
non-divine power working from within.

Now there are also some individuals in whom unwanted and
potentially dangerous bleedings occur that even all today's scientific advances can check with difficulty, if at all. A case in point
are haemophiliacs, born with blood that clots only very slowly,
so that they live in daily danger of literally bleeding to death as
a result of some quite trivial injury. So if crucifixion-type imaging
and a hypnotic state can cause an individual to bleed, can this
mysterious inner power be applied in reverse, and check a haemophiliac's uncontrollable bleeding?

Haemophilia is a genetic disorder, the result of a defective chromosome carried by women members of a family, but manifesting
itself exclusively in male offspring. It has affected a well-known
family line, that of the British Queen Victoria. Victoria was a carrier
of the defective chromosome, and no-one was to become more
acutely aware of this hidden legacy than her grand-daughter, Princess Alix of Hesse, who after marrying Tsar Nicholas II of Russia
gave birth to four healthy daughters, followed by one haemophiliac son, Alexei. Alexei stood to inherit the entire Russian Empire

and its one hundred million subjects – if he could somehow survive his dreadful disability.

It was a heart-rending situation for Alix, or the Empress Alexandra as she was now titled, and her husband. Sworn to secrecy about their patient's condition, the imperial doctors knew enough to recognise the signs of haemophilia in the young Alexei, but had no idea how to check any bleeding if this should occur. They could only recommend the most stringent measures to prevent Alexei suffering any falls, cuts or scratches. A huge sailor was deputed to guard him at all times, and to carry him in any circumstances where he had to remain on his feet for any length of time. Yet despite such precautions, every now and again the haemophilia flared, and the young Alexei's life hung in the balance.

While this situation was preoccupying the imperial family closeted in their court in St Petersburg, far to the east, in the wilds of western Siberia an unkempt and extraordinary 'holy man' called Grigorii Rasputin was coming to public notice. Although of the crudest peasant upbringing, lacking in religious vocation, and sexually licentious, Rasputin stemmed from a long Siberian tradition of wild men accredited with powers of spiritual and physical healing and second sight. Everyone who met him attested to the sheer animal magnetism that blazed from his eyes. As a result of his successes where conventional medicines had failed, he gradually began to percolate into the upper echelons of aristocratic society, particularly after seeming to cure from near-fatal fever the daughter of the Empress's lady-in-waiting, Lili Dehn.

It was merely a matter of time before Rasputin came to the attention of the credulous and superstitious Empress Alexandra. He was first summoned to help her when she was at her most frantic over one of Alexei's early attacks. Although we have no eye-witness evidence of what took place at Alexei's bedside on this occasion, there has survived a hearsay account from theatre director V. A. Telyakovsky. Accordying to Telyakovsky, on asking one of those he knew within the court circle about Rasputin, he was told:

> He's a strange one. He was taken to the bedside of the Tsarevich [i.e. Alexei] . . . The child looked at him and began to bubble with laughter. Rasputin laughed too. He laid his hand on the boy's leg and the bleeding stopped at once. 'There's a good boy,' says Rasputin. 'You'll be all right. But only God can tell what will happen tomorrow.'[1]

Anecdotal though it is, this account is almost certainly true in essence. There has never been any suggestion that Rasputin was able fully to clear Alexei's haemophilia. But time and again he seems to have been able to stop Alexei's bleeding attacks whenever these came on, and the distraught Alexandra repeatedly sought his aid. Even the imperial doctors and those who most detested him grudgingly acknowledged his successes in this regard.

So how did he do it? Just as we have found shifting and ill-defined states of hypnosis behind the manifestation of stigmata, so something of this kind seems to have been a factor the way Rasputin caused Alexei's bleeding to stop. It would be quite wrong to explain Rasputin merely as a hypnotist. Although hypnosis was well known in his time, he himself did not overtly practise it, his innocence of it being such that he actually enrolled for a course to learn about it some long while after his successes with Alexei.

But as one of several ways in which his behaviour resembled that of Jesus Christ (despite other obvious differences) Rasputin seems to have been so naturally hypnotic that he could naturally induce significant changes in the physical and psychological well-being of others. While to this day no-one properly understands how he achieved such effects, his ability was to have a profound influence on the history of Russia. His hold over the imperial family became so powerful that it was to be one of the contributory factors in the demise of the ruling Romanov dynasty and the birth of the Russian Revolution.

It is interesting also to note that as recently as the 1970s an American psychiatrist called Agle conducted hypnotic experiments on haemophiliac children and found, like Rasputin, that he too was able to dramatically reduce the frequency of the children's bleeding episodes.[2]

Self-hypnotic controls over blood supply continue to be exhibited to this day by those who, by way of entertainment in India and other eastern countries, pass long needles through their cheeks, tongues, and other parts of their bodies, yet show neither pain nor bleeding to anything like the extent that might be expected. In the course of a television programme on pain shown in the BBC's *Body Matters* series, one such individual who performs such feats, the great Orchante, was wired to an electro-encephalograph, or EEG machine, on which his brain rhythms registered the classic alpha wave pattern characteristic of a state of relaxed alertness as in, though not exclusive to, hypnosis.

If then there is something within us which can override our

autonomic body systems (and this is clearly of profound medical significance) what about actual flesh change among stigmatics? We may recall the strange gristle-like forms in St Francis of Assisi and others which were interpreted as the heads and bent-over points of crucifixion nails. Of St Francis the *Fioretti* author wrote:

> His hands and feet appeared to have been pierced through the centre by nails, the heads of which were in the palms of his hands and the soles of his feet, standing out from the flesh; and their points issued from the backs of the hands and feet, so that they seemed to have been bent back and clinched in such a fashion that a finger could easily have been thrust through the bend outside the flesh as though through a ring; and the heads of the nails were round and black.[3]

Of seventeenth century Italian stigmatic Giovanna Bonomi a beatification witness attested:

> the flesh of her hands stood out like the head of a nail.[4]

Of nineteenth century Tyrolean stigmatic Domenica Lazari medical specialist Dr Dei Cloche reported:

> About the centre of the exterior of her hands . . . there rose a black spot resembling the head of a large nail.[5]

Of Dorothy Kerin's hand-wounds, Brother William wrote that the marks in her hands and feet were:

> . . . as though pierced by the holy nails, bearing the impress of the head of same in the palms of her hands and the instep of her feet and the sharp point on the backs of her hands and the soles of her feet.[6]

If we accept that something with the stigmatics' metabolisms did reshape the substance of their bodies – and although it asks a lot, I find no legitimate reason for disbelieving this – and then envisage the process in reverse, it should theoretically be possible to harness this for purposes of physical healing. So are there any pointers that this may be so?

I do not propose to go into examples such as the faith-healing claims associated with Lourdes. While potentially relevant, these raise special difficulties of assessing their validity, and rarely have the backing of authoritative medical opinion.

But it is possible to find examples in orthodox medical literature which, though they defy normal medical explanation, are highly suggestive of the sort of power we are postulating, particularly as they involve hypnosis. In 1978 the medical journal *The Practitioner* published an account by Hampshire dermatologist Dr Richard Dreaper[7] of how he had used hypnosis to cure an intractable case of warts. Warts tend to appear and disappear unpredictably, regardless of treatment. But Dr Dreaper's case, because of the controls he used, seems to indicate hypnotic power working in a particularly striking way.

The patient, a fifty-six year old woman, had both hands severely disfigured by large, ugly warts. Conventional attempts to clear these, such as with tablets, with Salactol and liquid nitrogen, had all proved useless. It was decided as a last resort to try hypnosis. The woman proved a surprisingly good subject, and over a series of sessions her warts began to shrivel up.

Now because of the unpredictability of warts, it was possible that the hypnosis was coincidental to, and not the cause of, the cure. So to at least minimise this possibility, Dreaper suggested to the patient that after all other warts had disappeared one, on her right ring finger, would remain as a control. And indeed, this particular wart was the only one which obstinately remained. To further vindicate the point, when this wart was instructed to disappear, it did so. Two years later none of the warts had returned.

Compared to the stigmatic manifestation of nailheads, wart-removal is fairly insignificant. Is there any more dramatic example of whatever power might be involved? Indeed there is, and the case has been published and documented in orthodox medical literature.[8]

In 1950 a sixteen year old boy was admitted to the Royal Victoria Hospital, East Grinstead, Surrey suffering from ichthyosiform erythrodermia, a rare and particularly unsightly condition. Virtually his entire body was covered with a hard black horny substance resembling the skin of an armoured reptile. When touched this was as hard as a fingernail, but when stretched by minor bending it opened up into cracks which oozed a bloody serum. These became easily infected and painful and gave off an unpleasant smell, resulting in the boy being shunned by teachers and fellow-pupils alike.

The time was not long after World War II, during which severely disfiguring injuries had prompted major advances in plastic surgery, and it was decided to cut away some of the worst areas on the boy's body, and graft on skin from his chest, which was more normal. Two attempts of this kind were made, but each time the grafted skin rapidly took on the same reptilian appearance. Even the great pioneer of plastic surgery, Sir Archibald McIndoe, declared further attempts useless.

By chance the boy's plight came to the notice of a young physician with an interest in hypnosis, Dr A.A.Mason, today a psychoanalyst in Beverly Hills, California. Mason asked those treating the boy if he might try hypnosis, and on 10 February 1951 commenced this treatment, first inducing the hypnosis itself, then suggesting to the boy that his left arm's reptilian layer would disappear. To even Mason's astonishment an extraordinary transformation ensued. According to his medical report, as published in the *British Medical Journal*:

> About five days later the horny layer softened, became friable, and fell off . . . From a black and armour-like casing, the skin became pink and soft within a few days . . . At the end of ten days the arm was completely clear from shoulder to wrist.[9]

During the next few weeks Mason methodically gave hypnotic suggestions for the clearance of the reptilian layer on the right arm and then for specific remaining areas of his body, each time with between 50 and 95 per cent success.

The apparent substance of the 'reptile' skin, keratin, was most likely the same as that from which the stigmatics' horny 'nails' were created. If a hypnotic command could so effectively remove something as substantial as the horny armour that covered the boy, a reverse process might therefore have created features resembling nail-heads out of the same substance.

A further aspect of this impeccably attested case – Dr Mason kindly made available to me a complete set of his medical photographs – is that unknown even to Mason at the time (because of the condition's rarity), ichtyosiform erythrodermia is, like haemophilia, a congenital condition. As Mason freely acknowledges, had he known this at the time, he would not even have tried to treat the boy because he would have assumed hypnosis to be unable to tackle anything so deep-seated. Yet the hypnosis *did* work, as spectacular a change for the better as stigmatics' changes have been disfiguring.

If we are then prepared to accept that there really is a flesh-changing potential within us, what are its possible applications, and what its limits? One application for which claims have been made is cosmetic breast enlargement. There were some early experiments along these lines in 1948, but during the mid 1970s American practitioner R.D. Willard tried to put these onto a more scientific level in a research exercise involving twenty-two volunteer female subjects, ranging in age from nineteen to fifty-four.[10]

First a qualified physician made careful measurements of the women's breasts. Then, after each of the women had been lightly hypnotised, they were told to imagine warm water flowing over their breasts and the breasts becoming pleasantly warm. If they had difficulty imagining this, they were alternatively asked to think of a heat-lamp radiating on them, and causing these to pulsate. They were then given tape-recordings of hypnotic suggestions along similar lines, and asked to take these home and listen to them every day for twelve weeks. Regular check-ups were held during this period.

At the end, twenty of the twenty-two had achieved some enlargement, of whom nine needed to buy a bigger bra. Six had actually reached the size of breast that they had aimed for, and had ceased to follow the tape-recorded suggestions. The average size increase was about two thirds of an inch vertically, more than an inch horizontally, and 1.37 inches in circumference. Some women achieved almost twice these gains. Nor could these be attributed just to a general gain in weight, for nine women lost two pounds or more during the experiment. Among those who had had children and wanted firmer breasts there was a significant improvement.

One interesting feature of this and the ichthyosis case, in line with the imaging encountered in stigmatics, is the visualisation factor in a hypnotic state.

A very similar accent on visualisation, accompanied by relaxation techniques that are effectively the same as self-hypnosis, forms the keynote of the therapeutic approach to cancer and other diseases pioneered by Dr Carl Simonton and his wife Stephanie Matthews-Simonton of the Cancer Counseling and Research Center in Dallas, Texas, and subsequently adopted in the UK by well-respected alternative health ventures such as the Bristol Cancer Help Centre.

As set out in their best-selling book *Getting Well Again*,[11] the Simontons instruct their patients first to relax completely. The patients make themselves comfortable in a softly-lit room, breathing deeply and concentrating on every part of their bodies becoming released of tension. Then they are asked to visualise their body's own natural defences combating the cancer in the most vivid terms possible. According to the instructions:

Mentally picture the cancer in either realistic or symbolic terms. Think of the cancer as consisting of very weak, confused cells. Remember that our bodies destroy cancerous cells thousands of times during a normal lifetime ... Picture your body's own white blood cells coming into the area where the cancer is, recognising the abnormal cells, and destroying them. There is a vast army of white blood cells. They are very strong and aggressive ... Picture the cancer shrinking. See the dead cells being carried away by the white blood cells and being flushed from your body through the liver and kidneys and eliminated in the urine and stool ... Imagine yourself well, free of disease, full of energy.[12]

The Simontons offer their methods as complementary to, rather than competing with, chemotheraphy and other conventional treatments. So while they claim on average to double the life expectancy of those cancer patients whom they treat compared to those they do not, any statistical evaluation of their success is difficult. Nonetheless, some of their patients tell remarkably supportive stories. One, Bob Gilley, an insurance executive from Charlotte, North Carolina, has related how, after months of debilitating intensive chemotherapy for a cancer in the groin, becoming progressively weaker and without any sign of success, he happened to attend a Simonton clinic at Fort Worth. Even the visualisation programme on its own seemed to help him and give him straight away a spirit of optimism which he had previously been lacking. But far more spectacular was what followed. According to his own account:

No medical differences showed up for two, three, even four weeks. But I kept holding on to the belief that this system would work. After six weeks I was examined by my doctor in Charlotte. As he began probing my body, I can't begin to describe the absolute terror that came over me. 'Maybe it's spread!' I thought. 'Maybe it's five times bigger than it was before.' My doctor turned to me in amazement and said with a very tender expression. 'It's considerably smaller. As a matter of fact, I would say that it's shrunk seventy-five per cent in mass size.' We rejoiced together, but cautiously.

Two weeks later – which was only two months after I had met the Simontons – I was given a gallium scan and various other tests and examinations. There was absolutely no disease present, only a residual scar nodule about the size of a small marble. Within two months of beginning relaxation and imagery, I was cancer-free! My doctors in Charlotte didn't believe it.[13]

It is a story yet again of mind over matter, and similar can be quoted from the Bristol Cancer Help Centre in my own home city. Arguably we are seeing in this, along with the ichthyosis cure and similar, the reverse side of the coin to the manifestation of stigmata, but the same inner process. Whatever the process is, it may even be able to affect bone. This is a least suggested by the curious 'crown of thorns' skull formation of thirteenth century St Christina of Stommeln preserved at Nideck in France; also a distinctive skull ridging on the upper forehead in photographs of stigmatised blind Spanish Archibishop Clemente Dominguez. If valid, such examples might go some way towards an understanding of the knitting of bones reported in some faith healings.

But in a world that demands conclusive proof, it still takes a lot of believing. The situation is further complicated by the bizarreness of some of the other claims made of stigmatics, for instance being able to survive without food or drink, or being in two places at once. Are these just tall tales added on to the already near incredible? Or might there be anything genuine among them that can teach us more about the nature and limits of this strange inner power?

STRETCHED POTENTIALS –
OR CREDIBILITY?

DIFFICULT as it is to believe some of the flesh changes accredited to stigmatics, a plethora of other strange powers and faculties is attributed to them. Several are reported to have gone years without food or drink. Jane Hunt and Padre Pio are credited with powers of healing. Padre Pio and Therese Neumann were said to have appeared in visions to individuals hundreds of miles from where they were physically located at the time. So what is to be made of these claims?

There is a natural tendency for mind-boggling stories to attract further even taller tales. But it is intriguing how certain claims about stigmatics recur consistently over the centuries.

There is a good case for believing that the inner mechanism which triggers stigmata is the key to the heightening of a series of other potentials of the human body, not least of these being, the claimed power of certain stigmatics to extend or shrink their bodies, or parts of these, in more spectacular ways than the hypnotic breast enlargement noted in the last chapter.

For instance, in the sixteenth century, when Soeur Jeanne des Anges of Loudun so spectacularly performed as if possessed by devils, observing Englishmen Thomas Killigrew and Walter Montague both noted how her stomach swelled until it looked like that of a pregnant woman, her breasts inflated to the same proportion, and her tongue turned black and leathery-looking, and became, in Killigrew's words:

swollen to an incredible bigness, and never within her mouth from the first falling into her fit; I never saw her for a moment contract it.[1]

The arm of Italian sixteenth century stigmatic Blessed Stefana Quinzani reportedly grew longer while she was reliving the moment of Jesus being nailed to the cross. According to the account drawn up by twenty-one observing churchmen and noblemen, her right arm became:

> extended as if the hand were being really and immovably nailed, and at once the muscles are seen stretched and tense, the veins swell and the hand grows black, and just as if it were indeed being fastened with a material nail, she utters a terrible shriek, followed by a hideous moaning. Then the left is extended in a similar manner to the right, but stretched considerably beyond its natural length.[2]

Much the same was noted of St Catherine of Genoa: 'The arm grew more than half a palm longer than it was by nature'.[3] In the nineteenth century Marie-Julie Jahenny, having predicted what would happen, produced a whole variety of contractions and enlargements in the course of one performance. On Friday 1 October 1880, before summoned witnesses who included the redoubtable Dr Imbert-Goubeyre[4] and five others, her head seemed to shrink into her body to just above the level of her shoulders, her whole frame shrivelled into a sort of ball, each of her shoulders seemed to protrude at right-angles to her collarbone, the right side of her body enlarged while the left shrank to virtually nothing, and, just as in the case of Soeur Jeanne, her tongue swelled to enormous proportions. All this was in addition to her production of stigmata.

If one attempts a rational explanation of such instances, it may well be that they came about through unusual excitations and contractions of the body muscles and blood supply at the pertinent points. But the extraordinary factor is that the elusive inner mechanism seems to exhibit a command of systems normally well beyond conscious control. It seems not simply a case of mind over matter, but of activity by some agency beyond our normal conscious mind, overriding consciousness and the body's autonomic controls.

But what are the limits, if any, of this rarely manifested inner power? Here our only guide is to review the claims made of stigmatics over and above their actual stigmata, and to assess each to the best of our ability.

111

A repeated complaint among stigmatics has been their hyper-sensitivity to bright light, loud noises or strong smells. This was one reason why more than a few had to spend much of their lives shut away in darkened rooms. Such complaints have been commonly interpreted as hysteric over-reaction. Yet there are definite signs in certain stigmatics that, for instance, their hearing was genuinely so enhanced that a moderate noise would, to them, be quite deafening.

Thus in Allies, Pollen and Wynn's account of their visit to Domenica Lazzari, we find a direct reference to her hearing by Signor Yoris, the surgeon at Cavalese, the nearest main village. According to Yoris:

> I will tell you a curious instance of Domenica's acuteness of hearing. My wife and I were going once to visit her; when we were eighty or a hundred yards from her house, I whispered to my wife to go quietly, that we might take her by surprise. We did so accordingly, but much to our astonishment, she received us with a smile, saying that she had not been taken by surprise, and alluding to the very words I had used.[5]

As noted by Wynne:

> He [Yoris] showed us the spot where this had occurred, and it was certainly an acuteness of sense far beyond anything I can conceive possible.

Domenica was also said to have been able to hear what her parish priest was saying during his sermons in the local church, which was five or six hundred yards from where Domenica lived.

Another heightened potential often noted of stigmatics has been their need for minimal amounts of sleep. This applied to Padre Pio and others, including Dr Lechler's 'test' stigmatic, Elizabeth K. According to Lechler:

> For a few years now she [Elizabeth] has been able to do with two or three hours sleep per night despite fairly heavy physical work in the house and garden during the day. The explanation for this, according to Elizabeth herself, is that she tells herself not to be tired . . . Should she on occasion feel exhaustion, she tells herself: 'You are not tired, you are only imagining it' and her tiredness disappears immediately.[6]

Of all such claims, one of the most remarkable – and difficult to believe – has been the ability of certain stigmatics to subsist for years, even tens of years, on nothing more than Holy Communion. According to Dr Imbert-Goubeyre's statistics, one seventh of all stigmatics, mostly women, have had such claims made of them. The earliest known example is the Blessed Angela of Foligno, born in Assisi within a generation of the time of St Francis, who reputedly went twelve years without normal food. She was followed shortly after by St Catherine of Siena and the Blessed Elizabeth of Reute, both said to have fasted for a similar period, and in the sixteenth century by St Maria Maddalena de' Pazzi and Dominican nun Domenica of Paradise, who reputedly managed twenty years.

Nor did such claims diminish with the onset of the scientific age. Dr Imbert-Goubeyre noted that Marie-Julie Jahenny, showed a marked disinclination to eat from the onset of her stigmata. From 12 April 1874 she abstained altogether for ninety-four days. This was followed, on 28 December 1875, by the beginning of a claimed fast of no less than five years, one month and twenty-one days. According to Dr Imbert-Goubeyre's solemn attestation:

> Throughout all this period there was no excretion, either liquid or solid . . . The facts I adduce are genuine, beyond the reach of human fraud.[7]

Dr Imbert-Goubeyre also investigated and attested to the authenticity of similar claims made around the same time of Louise Lateau. From 1871 Louise was said to have refused any food except Holy Communion because it made her sick. Nonetheless she survived a further twelve years. Throughout this time, according to Dr Imbert-Goubeyre, she produced nothing from her bowels, and her urine output was no more than two spoonfuls a week, though her monthly periods were normal. In 1878 when she seemed near death, she was directly challenged by a Dr Lefebvre whether she could honestly attest before the tribunal of God that she had neither eaten nor drunk during the last seven years. According to Lefebvre, she replied very emphatically:

> In the presence of God who is to be my judge, and of the death I am expecting, I assure you that I have neither eaten nor drunk for seven years.[8]

Great caution is needed about such claims. For all his erudition, Dr Imbert-Goubeyre, who lived at Clermont Ferrand, hundreds of miles to the south of Marie-Julie and Louise, could never have kept up any serious long-term check on their bodily functions. This point is reinforced when we learn from Dr M. Warlomont,[9] one of those who conducted medical examinations on Louise Lateau, that a cupboard full of fruit and bread was found in her room.

Coming to the twentieth century, suspicion is also aroused by the claim made of Therese Neumann that she neither ate nor drank, except for a daily Communion wafer and a spoonful of water, from Christmas 1926 to the end of her life in 1962, a total of thirty-six years. Therese had a vigorous, stocky build throughout most of this time, and all reason tells us that it would be impossible to survive so long without food or drink.

Purportedly definitive tests that Therese really did live without normal food and drink were instituted by her local Bishop of Regensburg in July 1927. With the somewhat guarded agreement of the Neumann family – they refused to allow Therese to leave their house to go to any hospital – for fifteen days between the 14 and 28 July she was put under twenty-four hour observation by four fully qualified Franciscan nursing sisters under the supervision of a doctor.

The guidelines laid down were stringent. At least two nursing nuns were deputed to be with Therese at all times. The water with which she rinsed out her mouth was to be measured, along with all her bowel and urinary outputs. And she was to be repeatedly physically examined.

What followed was not entirely without incident. On the third night Therese seems to have overheard the nurses talking quietly about how the family's obstructiveness had made it difficult to carry out their duties exactly as instructed. According to biographer Poray Madeyski, Therese first went into a convulsive attack then, suddenly:

> began to listen, and declared that a voice had just told her that
> she must suffer for the four sisters, who were proving
> unworthy of the high task entrusted to them, since they
> expressed uncharitable opinions about the parish priest, about
> herself, and also about a man who had a part in all this and
> had an important role, but was an unbeliever . . .[10]

Subsequently Therese appears to have calmed down, and the rest of the fortnight proceeded straightforwardly enough. On a couple of occasions she was reported to have vomited mucus and blood mixed with gastric juices, but she was not observed to eat anything, neither did she produce any intestinal output.

At the beginning of the period she tipped the scales at 121 pounds. After the first of her Friday sufferings – which continued during the test period – this dropped to 112.5 pounds. Then it increased, to register after the second of her Friday bleeds at 115 pounds. By the fifteenth day she had returned to her original weight of 121 pounds.

Her urine output was measured and chemically tested during both the 14–28 July observation period and the fortnight after. The chart of this was as follows:

Date	15 July	21 July	26 July	5 August
Quantity	345 cc	180 cc	45 cc	75 cc
Reaction	Very acid	Acid	Acid	Neutral
Colour	–	–	Dark straw	Clear
Density	1025	1024	1033	1014
Chlorate of soda	0.657%	0.84%	1.08%	1.02%
Nitrogen	1.28%	2.245%	1.195%	0.482%
Acetone	V. strong	Strong	Trace	Absent
Acetic acid	1.7%	Traces	Slight trace	Absent
Creatinin	0.152%	0.24%	Trace	Trace[11]

This is particularly valuable for an understanding of Therese, for the picture for 15 July and 21 July is just what one would expect of complete fasting, with all the chemical indications of hunger after a period in which the body has been used to food. A tell-tale feature is the high build-up of acids.

But the picture for 5 August, after the twenty-four hour observations had been lifted, indicates a return to normal, suggesting that once Therese was no longer subject to round-the-clock observation, she went back to normal food and drink intake. Adding to this suspicion was the subsequent insistence by Therese and her family that the July 1927 test had been a once-and-for-all exercise which they were not prepared to repeat.

So was Therese a fraud, at least in respect of her food and drink intake? Within the last ten years there has been a deception of precisely this kind perpetrated by one Signorina Alfonsina Cottini from the tiny Alpine village of Craveggio, near Lake Maggiore, northern Italy.[12] In her late sixties Alfonsina retired permanently to bed, letting it be known that she had abandoned all eating and drinking, and that all her bowel and bladder functions had stopped. She carried this off so convincingly that for ten years coachloads of credulous pilgrims would come to see her reclining beatifically on her iron bed, surrounded by hundreds of photographs and other mementoes of her previous visitors.

Then stories began to circulate around Craveggio that Alfonsina's sister was amassing large sums of money, and that at night Alfonsina would get up, raid the fridge and perform the other necessities of life. The church authorities set up a special commission and found the village's darkest suspicions correct. Not least of their discoveries was that Alfonsina produced eliminations 'of a remarkable potency'.

It would be easy for similar charges to be levelled against Therese Neumann, not least because, like Alfonsina, she created a comfortable tourist industry for the Neumann family and for Konnersreuth. One well-wisher even provided her with her own specially heated chair for when she attended church. But the picture is not quite so simple. In Therese's defence her biographer Anni Spiegl, who spent many weeks living with the Neumann family, has vigorously insisted that she really did live without eating and drinking:

> I cannot imagine that it is possible to eat in secret for thirty-six years. Without thinking, one would be sure to put something into one's mouth automatically at some time or another. After all, Therese did not live shut away in a room all on her own, she was continually among people, was invited out a lot, often on journeys and with people of a different faith. Nor was Therese of a delicate build which would have managed with little to eat . . . Furthermore, to put it plainly, anyone who eats also excretes and both cannot be kept secret for decades – for decades Therese had not passed excretions of any kind. I spent ten weeks in Therese's permanent company and could enter her room at any time without knocking; I also helped clean her room and should certainly have come across any food hidden there since from working in a shop one becomes alert and quick to notice things, it comes from the job. I often lived with Therese for weeks on end in Eichstätt, I packed and unpacked her little suitcase with her and never saw anything suspicious.[13]

The plain fact is that no fraud was ever actually discovered on Therese's part. So what is the answer? It seems likely that, besides the other heightened potentials we have noted, stigmatics have been genuinely able to go for unusually long periods with little or no food, but to nothing like the extent claimed of them.

Certainly there is something odd about stigmatics' food intake. Padre Pio, who never claimed to abstain from food and drink, nonetheless ate extraordinarily sparingly for the solid build he assumed in maturity. As noted by his biographer Charles Carty,[14] he took only one meal a day, at noon, comprising vegetables with perhaps a little fish or cheese, in all no more than three or four hundred calories against the two thousand required for minimal physical exertion. Like Therese Neumann, when once he ate nothing for eight days because of stomach trouble, he was found to have actually gained weight during this time.

Dr Lechler, although emphatically no supporter of Therese Neumann, happened to note in the course of his observations of Elizabeth K.:

> During her illness when she refused food for six weeks and had to be force-fed I had noticed that she had not lost weight, but in fact had gained half a pound. With the small amount of food given to her, a normal person would have lost considerable weight. When I pointed this out to her under hypnosis she told me that she was frightened she might die if she lost weight, and she kept telling herself 'I must not lose weight'.
>
> In order to research further into her metabolism, I suggested to her to put on seven pounds during the following week. This suggestion was repeated several times. At the end of the week she had indeed gained seven pounds although her food intake had remained the same and she had carried out her daily work.[15]

So with the qualification that there may have been an element of duplicity in the case of Therese – perhaps one of her personalities, in all truthfulness, fasted, while another, like Alfonsina, crept out at night to raid the larder – we seem yet again to be looking at some form of heightened potential. And other stories about stigmatics suggest yet more extended powers.

One such concerns repeated claims of second sight among stigmatics, particularly in regard to sensing the deaths of individuals around them. Such stories were told of the earlier stigmatics and of Therese Neumann, and also among the English stigmatics of our own time.

According to Ted Harrison, the BBC journalist who interviewed

Ethel Chapman, she not uncommonly had premonitions of the deaths of fellow residents at her Springwood Cheshire Home, and also of members of her family. These were often signalled by unexpected bleedings from her stigmata. In her own words:

About three years ago, just after I came, there was the first death. My hands bled the night before.[16]

She was very ready to point out that a death had been expected in the home on that particular occasion, but this was not the case in an earlier occurrence:

Two years ago there was another death and it wasn't expected at all. My hands bled very heavily that night, just the night before. The gentleman went into hospital and nobody had any idea he was so poorly, in fact the staff here didn't realise that it was dehydration and he passed away. It was a shock to everybody, even the doctors and the staff in the home. As my hands were bleeding I did not know who my hands were bleeding for. I don't always know. But if there's someone ill in the home, yes I do know'.[17]

Jane Hunt told me how one night while receiving one of her messages from Jesus she seemed to see standing by the side of the bed a man whom she did not know, along with, quite incongruously, a tortoise on top of the wardrobe. When a friend phoned her to tell her that the friend's father had died in the night, Jane enquired the time of his death. It turned out to be the same as when she had received her vision. Jane went on:

And then she [the friend] brought a photo. And I said: 'That's the man that was here, at the bed.' And that was the father. And I'd never met him.[18]

The tortoise came to be explained in the same way. Unable to get the creature out of her mind, Jane decided to phone a neighbour who owned a tortoise to ask if it was all right. The neighbour told her: 'Of course, yes, we fed him not long ago. He's fine.'
But Jane persisted:

I said: 'Can you have another look?' And she said: 'Well, he hasn't eaten anything. There's all his food there.' And the husband picked him up, and the tortoise was dead. And I just felt that I knew about it.

Of the same order are instances of stigmatics seeming to transcend space. Teresa Higginson professed on one occasion to have been transported to a country she supposed to be Africa, finding herself among a primitive people whose habits and customs she described in great detail.[19] Therese Neumann was reputedly seen by Father Ingbert Naber, of the Capuchin Monastery at Eichstätt, one day when he had to preach a special mission in Eichstätt. Therese was apparently clearly visible to him for three quarters of an hour, standing in the back of the meeting in her black dress and characteristic white head-cloth. Yet she had never left Konnersreuth. She had simply told her sister Ottilie: 'Today Father Ingbert begins his mission. We'll have to pray real hard for him.'[20]

But the most spectacular are the stories about Padre Pio. One individual particularly deeply impressed by these has been John McCaffery. He was chief of the Swiss headquarters of Special Operations Europe during World War II, and subsequently became one of Padre Pio's biographers. He has accepted, among many others, an extraordinary tale of the padre healing at a distance, as was told to him by a young Paduan farmer whom he met on a train journey.

As a result of a serious accident when still young the farmer had developed embolisms in both lungs which conventional medicine had failed to cure. Of Catholic upbringing, and realising that he was facing death, he prayed as never before for someone to intercede on his behalf. Whereupon, according to his own account:

I had what I can only describe as an apparition. There was a bearded monk by my bedside. He bent forward and laid his hand on my chest, smiled, and then disappeared.[21]

Although cured, the farmer felt too embarrassed to tell how this had happened to anyone but his mother, until he was entertained to lunch in a businessman's home several months later, when he noticed on the wall a photograph which he recognised as that of the monk who had appeared to him. Learning that this was Padre Pio (at that time relatively unknown), the farmer that very evening took the train to Foggia, the nearest station for San Giovanni Rotondo. On attending Padre Pio's early morning Mass he confirmed beyond doubt that Padre Pio had been the monk of his vision. Yet more extraordinary was to follow when, later that day, he was able to make his Confession with Padre Pio. He told McCaffery:

Here and now in the train ... I relive, I assure you, all the emotion of that moment. He blessed me, and I made my Confession. And then, at the end of it, he said to me with the most natural voice in the world: 'And tell me, what about the lungs now? How are they?' 'Thank you, Father,' I answered him, 'They are perfect.' 'Have you had them X-rayed?' 'Yes, Father.' 'Good, thanks be to God. And God bless you.' Do you wonder that I keep going down to San Giovanni? Or that it gives me goose-flesh to recount these things to you even now?

Another such story is told by Italian journalist Giovanni Gigliozzi. One day shortly before an important radio broadcast, he was struck with such a blinding migraine – a problem to which he was prone – that he feared he would be unable to do the programme. Implored by the station director to try to get rid of the migraine by a quick rest, he had settled onto a couch at the studios when he seemed to be aware of someone approaching accompanied by a click of rosary beads. On looking up, there was an apparition of Padre Pio who simply smiled, laid his hand on his head, and left. Immediately Gigliozzi found himself cured. He was so impressed that that very Sunday he travelled to San Giovanni Rotondo and during the evening knelt before Padre Pio while the latter was in conversation with his fellow friars. Turning to him, Padre Pio asked: 'Well Giovanni, and how is the head?' 'Thank you, Padre', Giovanni responded. 'Very well indeed.' 'Ah', muttered Pio with a knowing smile, 'These hallucinations ...'[22]

Another persistent story is that of stigmatics seeming to register their presence, sometimes after death, or when hundreds of miles away, in the form of a mysterious perfume. Such was reported of the eighteenth century Italian stigmatic nun St Maria Francesca of the Five Wounds, who was said to have imparted something of her fragrance to everything she touched. According to her nineteenth century biographer Laviosa:

There is hardly one of the numerous witnesses [espousing the cause of her beatification] ... who does not speak in explicit terms of this perfume, and in order that there might be no doubt that the favour came to her from her Mother Mary and from her divine spouse [i.e. Christ], it was regularly observed that this phenomenon manifested itself with special intensity on the great festivals of our Lady and on the Fridays in March on which she participated mysteriously in the sufferings of Christ's Passion.[23]

There are numerous perfume stories of Padre Pio, some being experienced many hundreds of miles from where Padre Pio was physically located in San Giovanni Rotondo. One such story concerns a Polish couple who lived in England, and who had a special difficulty which they outlined in a letter to Padre Pio. Receiving no reply – as earlier noted, he was forbidden to write letters to the outside world   they decided to journey to San Giovanni Rotondo to talk to him in person. During their journey they stayed in a particularly dilapidated hotel, but to their surprise instead of their room smelling of damp, it seemed to be delightfully perfumed, although they could find no trace of the source of this fragrance. When they eventually reached San Giovanni Rotondo and met Padre Pio, they apologised for coming without an appointment, explaining that they had written but received no replay.

To their astonishment Padre Pio responded indignantly:

How do you mean I did not reply? That evening at the inn,
did you smell nothing?[24]

Padre Pio's biographer John McCaffery has also attested to this same perfume:

Did I ever experience it? Time and again, alone, in company,
in San Giovanni and far away from it – but always completely
unexpectedly, and therefore with no possibility of auto-
suggestion. It generally conveyed a message, but sometimes
was just like an affectionate pat on the head . . .[25]

Could it be that the stretched potentials of the stigmatic include an ability to transmit something of the personality, visually, or by means of a perfume, over distances of hundreds of miles? One question this raises is how the stigmatic manages to cope with being in two places at once.

This dilemma was deftly broached to Padre Pio by his long-time friend Dr Sanguinetti, the medical director of the hospital which he initiated at San Giovanni Rotondo. The conversation was recorded by Sanguinetti:

Sanguinetti: Padre Pio, when God sends a saint, for instance
like St Anthony[26] to another place by bilocation, is that person
aware of it?

> *Padre Pio*: Yes. One moment he is here and the next moment
> he is where God wants him.
> *Sanguinetti*: But is he really in two places at once?
> *Padre Pio*: Yes.
> *Sanguinetti*: How is this possible?
> *Padre Pio*: By a prolongation of his personality.[27]

In all this a large measure of caution is needed. Just how easily
tall stories can be created around stigmatics is demonstrated by
a tale told by English Catholic priest Father Michael Hollings of
an incident he personally observed while acting as server at one
of Padre Pio's masses. There came the point in the ritual at which
the priest breaks the main, celebratory mass wafer, which he is
then supposed to eat, either in whole or part. As recalled by Hollings:

> Padre Pio's hands were sore. He broke the host and the host
> fell into the chalice [the vessel for the wine].
> I saw the host in the chalice when I gave him water for the
> ablutions after the Communion, and there it was. As soon as
> we arrived out of the church afterwards, my companion and
> I, everyone said: 'Miraculo! Miraculo!' So we said: 'Why?' 'The
> host was there, and then it was gone!' So we said: 'No, it
> wasn't.' And so a miracle had occurred, which in fact had not
> occurred.[28]

What also has to be acknowledged is that when some stigmatics
tell stories about themselves, the characteristic simplistic quality
of their mentality gives them an unguarded lack of concern for
the hard factuality of what may have happened, though they have
no intention to deceive. Jane Hunt, for instance, in her television
interview quite emphatically told Ted Harrison that she had
received her stigmata on the very day that she went to her father
to forgive him for the way he had abused her in childhood. And
on this same day, St James' Day, she also said she had shown
the wounds to her vicar. Finding it difficult to put a time sequence
to all this, I asked her if she could give an hour by hour account
of what had happened. I was told that the call on her father had
actually been some weeks before, and learned from the vicar that
he was not shown Jane's hands on the St James Day evening,
but on the following Sunday morning. Of course everyone's
memory is fallible but it should be recognised that the stigmatic's

order of reality is not necessarily the same as the layman's. In them the borderline between trance state and normal consciousness is strangely blurred.

Despite these reservations, it seems undeniable that there is something about stigmatics 'beyond our ken'. So how, given all that we have seen, are we finally to assess them?

STIGMATA IN PERSPECTIVE

IN the light of all that we have seen throughout this book, there can be no easy overall assessment of the phenomenon of stigmata. The facile view would be to stress the diversity of wounds, indicating the unlikelihood that they are replications of the wounds of Christ, and the high incidence of the phenomenon among women of neurotic disposition, and dismiss it all as an imperfectly understood psychosomatic disorder. But this would fail to come to grips with the profound questions the fact of stigmata raises.

Without denying the genuineness and intensity of the religious faith of many stigmatics, their wounds are not to be interpreted either as miraculous or as signs of divine favour. Their very diversity defeats the claim that they replicate the original injuries suffered by Jesus. And many stigmatics have been notable more for their neuroses than their sanctity.

Nor should such an assessment offend anyone's religious faith, for even the Roman Catholic Church has adopted extreme caution and scepticism towards stigmatics throughout much of its history. A comparatively small proportion of stigmatics have been beatified or canonised. A saint – such as St Francis was very justifiably acclaimed – may be a stigmatic, but a stigmatic is by no means necessarily a saint.

Once the religious issue, which has obscured the subject for too long, is set aside, the real enigma is that stigmata really do happen, even in England, and even in the twentieth century. There are stigmatics living today in England, the USA, Italy, Spain and elsewhere. Shy and retiring though many of them are, their flesh really does change in a manner all too similar to that attested of better-known stigmatics down the centuries. Whatever the truth of claimed accompaniments such as living without eating or drinking, those who manifest stigmata also exhibit some mysterious side-effects. Even allowing for fraud and myth-making, the phenomenon clearly has further unplumbed depths.

We appear to be dealing with an extraordinarily profound inner mechanism, and some indication of this, hitherto unremarked, is the common age at which some stigmatics have died.

It may be recalled how stigmata often exhibit a chronological precision in their appearance, as if to the command of an inner clock. Sometimes it is a particularly regular time of day, often it is a special day of the week, most notably Friday, the day of Jesus's crucifixion. It may be a special anniversary such as Easter. St Francis became stigmatised on the Feast of the Holy Cross, Padre Pio's bleeding began during the octave of the Feast of St Francis's stigmatisation. Jane Hunt favoured the feast of the patron saint of her local church, St James.

Could an inner clock determine even the year in which stigmatics would die? Interesting in this regard has been the widespread belief, before New Testament scholarship complicated the picture, that Jesus lived for thirty-three years. The popular supposition was that he was born in 0 AD and died in 33 AD. We know this to be wrong, not least because Herod the Great, in whose reign Jesus was born, died in 4 BC. However, a small but significant proportion of stigmatics own span of life was indeed thirty-three years. Even allowing for coincidence, it seems more than chance that about thirty-three years was the death age of Lukardis of Oberweimar, St Catherine of Siena, Mother Agnes of Jesus, Madeleine Morice, Domenica Lazzari, Louise Lateau and Teresa Musco. This list is by no means comprehensive. Could something within all these women have willed them to die at ostensibly the same age as their Saviour? Anthropologists attest that Australian aborigines can often die without apparent physical cause simply because they believe they have been programmed by some magic bone-pointing or curse.

So it seems this inner power is potent even unto death. We may have to accept that much of its nature will continue to elude us, but from all that we have seen, can we at least try to formulate it?

First, we can say with some confidence that the mechanism seems to be brought into play by extreme stress. A recurring feature of stigmatics' case histories is some severe shock such as a serious fall, a near-fatal illness, or the death of one or both parents. There also recur the extremes of fasting and mortification which many stigmatics have inflicted on their bodies.

Second, a recurring feature among stigmatics is the variety of altered states of mind that may be broadly labelled dissociated consciousness. These may take the form of trances, hysterical catalepsies, loss of sensation in parts of the body, blindness, loss of hearing, paralysis, and other dissociated states, particularly seeing visions, hearing voices and receiving other hallucinatory impressions. Time and again these visions and auditory experiences can be traced to religious stories the stigmatic has heard. The stigmatic, while in the dissociated state, reacts to these as if they were real. It cannot be emphasised enough that these visions are not incidental to the stigmatic phenomenon, they are integral to it, as if part of the programming into a different form of reality.

This leads to the third feature, the flesh-change denoting the stigmata proper. If we are indeed dealing with some inner mechanism it would seem to be at its most powerful at the recipient's ectodermal, or 'outer shell' level, hence the fact of comparatively few stigmatic phenomena being more than skin-deep. Here a really riveting feature is the extraordinary precision of the mechanism's conformity to the visualisations that triggered it. Stigmata have been precisely positioned to conform with the wounds of a stigmatic's favourite crucifix. Or a wound may have taken on an exact shape such as a cross. Most dramatic of all, the mechanism seems able to mould the flesh into a feature resembling the head and bent-over point of an iron nail. It is as if something within the body has re-programmed it into a new form, something normally quite impossible.

It is most unlikely that a mechanism of this kind has come into being simply to satisfy the whims of one particular brand of men and women who wanted to identify with the crucifixion agonies of the historical Jesus. You do not even need to be Christian, or in any way religious, to manifest flesh changes of a stigmatic kind. So could the mechanism have some more fundamental purpose within the order of nature?

As to what this might be, speculation is unavoidable. There is something about Dr Mason's ichthyosis case which seems to provide an important pointer. It would seem not unreasonable that the underlying cause of the boy's reptile or fish-skin could be a sort of Mendelian evolutionary throw-back of the kind whereby, for example, every now and again a black chicken or black sheep is born from a long-established line of white forebears. Another instance of this is the surprising numbers of the human population born with webbed feet, seemingly a harking back to part of our evolutionary past spent in the sea.

As we know from Dr Mason's report on his cure of the boy, the extraordinary flesh-change from reptilian to human was achieved by hypnotic suggestion.

Ever since Darwin published his theory of evolution there has been persisting disquiet that the theory of development of species from random mutations and natural selection still fails to satisfactorily explain the breath-taking diversity and complexity of life on this planet. The fossil-record shows that the path of evolution was not the slow, steady continuum one might expect from Darwinian theory, but has been characterised by surprising jumps after long periods of stability. These jumps or leaps in development seem to have occurred at times of stress upon individual species such as climatic change or threat from predators.

So strong is the case for these jumps that a whole new school for the theory has gathered around one of its leading proponents, Harvard University's Stephen Jay Gould.[1] But what the so-called punctuated equilibrium theory lacks is any adequate explanation for such short, sharp upheavals. How, for instance, could the dog-sized Eohippus, ancestor of the horse, have gone through the radical transformation into the modern creature in the few steps geologically indicated? Originally it was anticipated that fresh fossil discoveries would fill in the 'missing links', but this has not been the case.

So could species have made from within themselves dramatic changes of form at times of severe threat? And if so, how did they do it? In normal circumstances such things are impossible. Nor would it be desirable for one species member consciously to grow, say, some form of horn with which to terrorise the others of his kind in order to gain an individual advantage.

But what about circumstances of stress, when perhaps the whole species is threatened by some terrifying, hysteria-inducing newcomer, or other danger from without? Could there then be triggered some inner power, or underlying survival mechanism which permits the development of a new characteristic to tip the scales in favour of survival?

Here, it seems to me that the stigmatic/multiple personality mechanism just might offer a plausible key: an inner mechanism, activating only in circumstances of stress, capable of significant changes to the outward form according to whatever may be visualised.

Such a mechanism would also explain something that, to me at least, has always seemed baffling: how certain butterflies have evolved wing markings like large staring eyes to frighten predators; and how creatures such as thorn bugs, leaf and stick insects have developed bodies that, for purposes of protective camouflage, so exactly resemble their surroundings. To expect mere chance mutations and natural selection to produce such perfect mimicking seems to me like expecting any number of million monkeys armed with typewriters to produce a single play of Shakespeare. But if creatures, in certain circumstances, can change their colour, features or outward form, according to a visualised pattern, this seems to offer a glimmer more sense.

Tentative as such a hypothesis must be in our present state of knowledge, it is but one of many tantalising avenues of enquiry which the subject of stigmata opens up, if the scientific world recognises it as an area of legitimate inquiry, and the credulous accept that it is not the miraculous religious phenomenon they would like it to be. If only the myths can be cast aside, there is much more to be learned about stigmata and the subject should be investigated while we have among us individuals who exhibit the phenomenon.

Why, for instance, have so many stigmatics come from small, isolated rural communities, and so few from large cities? Are rustic populations more credulous? Or is it that city life, with its materialism and world weariness, dulls the faculty that becomes activated in the stigmatic? The issue undoubtedly needs further investigation.

Another question raised by stigmatics is whether they have anything in common physiologically. Interviewing Jane Hunt, I was struck by certain facial similarities, not least a common heaviness to the lower eyelids, to the photographs of Therese Neumann. Similar affinities could be noted of Ethel Chapman and Padre Pio. Have these similarities arisen because they have become stigmatics, or because they are of a type with a predisposition to becoming stigmatic? Again, further investigation is needed.

Another intriguing feature is the way individuals have become stigmatic seemingly because they have closely identified with previous stigmatics and mystics bearing the same name. Catarina, later Maria Maddalena de' Pazzi, for instance, seems to have sought to emulate her predecessor and namesake St Catherine of Siena. Therese Neumann seems to have chosen for her life model Thérèse of Lisieux, vaunted as the contemporary paragon of saintliness in Therese Neumann's formative years. Teresa Higginson may have been influenced by her namesake St Teresa of Avila. Padre Pio's original name was Francesco, he chose the Franciscan order as his vocation, and he became stigmatised within the octave of the Feast of St Francis of Assisi's stigmatisation. Something seems to have driven him to identify with his famous and saintly namesake to the very ultimate. Such identification with someone else and/or their sufferings – and obviously Jesus Christ was the ultimate model – seems to be a characteristic of the stigmatic, and again warrants further study.

Perhaps the most interesting question of all raised by stigmatics, and the one we have been able to study least, has been their apparent bursting of the normal bounds of our physical nature. It appears that our very bodies may be able to be changed by means other than surgery and drugs, and that we may even be able to transcend space. Did Padre Pio really achieve the at-a-distance healing described in the last chapter? Does Jane Hunt have a similar power? Could Ethel Chapman really sense the impending deaths of others? Such issues are fascinating, but they are so involved that they are beyond the scope of this book, and deserve more exhaustive study on their own.

What we have been able in a limited way to achieve in this book is to dispel much of the ignorant mythology surrounding stigmatics. Disappointing though it might be to some, it is no service to truth to perpetuate the belief that all stigmatics are saints, miraculously imprinted with the wounds of crucifixion exactly as suffered by Jesus Christ two thousand years ago. The evidence tells us that this cannot be so.

Nevertheless, stigmata are a fact, and remain a genuine mystery: the flesh really does change, and the reported accompaniments to the phenomenon may have a great deal to teach us.

Stigmata, whatever their origination, deserve to be taken seriously. If they are as spontaneous and particularised as they seem, they are one of the most baffling and intriguing of medical and scientific mysteries. If they are as far-reaching in their effects as we have shown, they demand a fundamental reappraisal of our understanding of the laws of nature. They offer us the potential of dramatic new insights into the development of all life. Most important of all, if the inner power that seems to generate them truly exists and can be better understood and harnessed, they perhaps promise opportunities for the cure of diseases that have so far defeated the best efforts of modern medicine.

Could one ask for more?

Appendix

STIGMATIC BIOGRAPHIES

The names are in chronological order, from St Francis of Assisi to the present day.

The Thirteenth Century

ST FRANCIS OF ASSISI (1181/2–1226) Born in Assisi, the son of Pietro Bernadone, a wealthy peripatetic cloth merchant. Gallant, high-spirited and generous during early years, living life of ease, and assisting father in his business. In 1202 taken prisoner during border dispute between Perugia and Assisi, suffering captivity for some months. On return to Assisi was overcome by serious illness, in the course of which he rejected the wordly life and decided to devote himself to the service of the poor. In ruined church of San Damiano had experience of Christ seeming to speak to him from crucifix, urging him to repair the church. In 1206 broke links with his father by publicly stripping himself of his fine clothes during legal dispute held before Bishop Guido of Assisi. Subsequently adopted extreme poverty in life and dress, giving rise in 1210 to approval of the Franciscan Order by Pope Innocent III. In September 1224, while spending a retreat on the wild slopes of Monte Alvernia, experienced a vision of Christ crucified, following which stigmatic wounds, the earliest positively known, appeared in his hands, feet and right side. These were still apparent on his death two years later. Also suffered hypersensitivity to light, sound etc. yet had apparent ability to desensitise himself against pain.

BLESSED DODO OF HASCHA (?–1231) Premonstratensian monk of Hascha in Frisia, who died when a ruined wall fell on him in 1231. When his body was brought out it was reported to have open wounds in the hands, feet and right side.

ST LUTGARDE OF TONGRES (1182–1246) Born at Tongres in Brabant, Cistercian nun who suffered apparent 'bloody sweat' of Gethsemane, when in one of her ecstasies blood from her hands and feet seemed to bathe her body.

BLESSED HELEN OF VESZPRIM (?–c. 1249) Nun of strictly enclosed Dominican Convent of Veszprim, Hungary. Stigmatised, first in her right hand, on Feast of St Francis (4 October) not later than 1237. Subsequently received wound in the side.

EMILA BICCHERI (1238–1278) From Vercelli, Piedmont. Exhibited only crown of thorns.

ST CHRISTINA OF STOMMELN (1242–1312) Received stigmata for the first time in 1268, her wounds, in hands, feet, forehead and side, subsequently bleeding every Easter. St Christina refused to discuss them, the wound in the side, for instance, only being observed because her dress was seen to be freshly blood-stained on the left side in the region of the heart. Her skull, preserved at Nideck, France, is said to have a curious bone formation, in the form of a fingers-breadth increase at the back proceeding towards the ears, almost like an additionally-grown circlet. It also has a series of regular markings, seemingly deriving from when she was alive, and suggestive of indentations made by a crown of thorns.

BLESSED ANGELA OF FOLIGNO (1250–1309) Born at Foligno near Assisi, was married, then widowed and lost all her children. She sold everything she owned, gave the money to the poor and joined the Third Order of St Francis. Stigmatised, she experienced frequent ecstatic visions, including one of Mary giving her the infant Jesus to hold in her arms. First known example of so-called inedia, she was said to have lived twelve years without food, after a Communion brought to her by angels. She was beatified by Pope Innocent XII in 1693.

BLESSED VANNA OF ORVIETO (1264–1306) Dominicaness of the Third Order. Received wound in the side only.

ELIZABETH OF HERKENRODE (d. 1275) Cistercian nun of Herkenrode, near Liège. Re-enacted whole Passion every twenty-four hours, striking herself fearful blows in the course of this.

HELENA BRUMSIN (d. 1285) Dominican nun of the enclosed convent of St Catherine at Diessenhofen, Thurgau. Bore only marks of scourging.

LUKARDIS OF OBERWEIMAR (c. 1276–1309) Was prone to repeated ecstasies, and received stigmata at an early stage, although for the two years prior she had the habit of driving her fingernails into her palms, and also subsequently dug her toes into wounds in her feet. Her stigmatisation reportedly appeared every Friday, the wounds remaining dry the rest of the week. She lived approximately thirty-three years.

The Fourteenth Century

ST CATHERINE OF SIENA (1347–80) She first felt the apparent pain of the Passion in 1373, with the sensation of a crown of thorns being pressed on her head. In the spring of 1375, when she was twenty-eight years old, she was reputedly stigmatised with the five wounds but then prayed that these should disappear, leaving her with the pain only, a wish that was apparently granted. She declined all food from the age of twenty, and would be sick when any was forced on her. On her death stigmata was said to have been traceable by a sort of transparency in the tissues. Lived thirty-three years.

ST RITA OF CASCIA (1381–1457) Augustinian nun from Roccaporena in the Apennines. Married for eighteeen years, then after husband's death entered the Augustinian convent at Cascia. In 1443, while praying before a crucifix, she felt herself pierced as if by a ray from Jesus' crown of thorns, and subsequently began bleeding from the forehead. Unusually for a stigmatic, these wounds later turned septic, but when this problem threatened to prevent her going to Rome for the Jubilee of 1450, they apparently miraculously disappeared.

BLESSED ELIZABETH OF REUTE (c. 1386–1420). Stigmatic said to have lived more than fifteen years without food.

The Fifteenth Century

ST LIDWINA OF SCHIEDAM (?–1433) A walking museum of ailments. Said to have eaten nothing for twenty-eight years.

ST CATHERINE OF GENOA (1447–1510) Born Caterinetta Fieschi, the daughter of a noble family of Liguria, northern Italy, Catherine married at the age of sixteen. After ten years of a pleasure-seeking existence, she developed a new spiritual attitude, and succeeded in converting her husband to the same frame of mind, the couple in partnership adopting a life of caring for the sick in a Genoa hospital. Although Catherine, unlike her husband, joined no religious order, she manifested remarkable religious experiences. Exceptional heat was reported from her stigmatic blood, and elongation of her arm during agonies preceding her death. In 1512, two years after her death, her body was said to have been found incorrupt, apparently remaining on display in this condition to this day.

BLESSED STEFANA QUINZANI (1457–1530) From Soncino, near Bergamo,

Italy. During complete re-enactment of the Passion every Friday, would exhibit bloody tears and sweat of Gethsemane. Crown of thorns also seen, and elongation of left arm as accompaniment of apparent nailing to the cross.

JOHANN JETZER (c. 1483–c. 1515) Son of a poor Catholic farmer from the tiny village of Zurzach, in the Swiss canton of Argovie (Aargau). Although minimally educated, in 1506, at the age of twenty-three, Jetzer presented himself at the Dominican friary of Berne for admission as a lay brother, apparently oiling the wheels of his acceptance by a hand-some gift of gold, jewels and finery for the Prior. Not long after his admission mysterious bangs, knocks, and poltergeist phenomena began to manifest around the friary, and Jetzer began seeing the loathsome apparition of a former Prior, one Heinrich Kalpurg, who had apparently deserted the friary, gone to Paris, fallen into evil company, and been murdered about a century and a half before. The Prior, purportedly in Purgatory, demanded Masses and various mortifications of Jetzer, who duly complied. After various subsequent visitations, the Prior one day appeared to Jetzer apparently restored to his rightful place in heaven. Jetzer's next claimed spectral visitors were first St Barbara, then the Virgin Mary, who conveyed to him the falsity of the Immaculate Conception doctrine that was being debated, but opposed by the Dominicans, at that time. Mary purportedly stigmatised Jetzer in the hands, and in sub-sequent visitations told him that he would receive the other wounds also, which duly manifested, accompanied by contortions and catalepsies in apparent simulation of Jesus's Passion. Further phenomena continued to beset Jetzer, including a weeping image of Mary, as a result of which he was summoned before a court of enquiry conducted by the Benedic-tine Bishop, Aymon de Montfaucon at Lausanne, commencing 8 October 1507. During the course of this Jetzer made various claims, then in November asserted that they were all false. As a result of the confusion and intense public interest, four leading figures within the friary were questioned under torture, ultimately confessing to various deceptions for which they were burnt at the stake. In the case of Jetzer, while he was awaiting judgment his mother smuggled in some female garments, and dressed in these he managed to slip out of prison and eventually escape from Berne. He subsequently married, and for the few remaining years of his life took up his old tailoring trade.

BLESSED OSANNA ANDREASI OF MANTUA (d. 1505) Nun of third Order of St Dominic. Received crown of thorns 24 February 1476, wound in the side the following June, and nail-wounds in hands and feet on Good Friday 1478. Her well preserved body is said still to show the marks of the stigmata.

MAGDALENA DE LA CRUZ (1487–post 1545) Spanish Franciscan-educated nun. Claimed stigmata and abstention from food, but confessed to cheating after becoming dangerously ill in 1543.

CLARE DE BUGNY (1471–1514) Tertiary of the Seraphic Order. Gushing, reputedly sweet-smelling side-wound studied by the Padua School of Medicine. Born on 4 October, the Feast of St Francis; died in Venice 17 September, the Feast of St Francis's stigmata.

The Sixteenth Century

DOMENICA OF PARADISE (1473–1555) Dominican nun whose stigmata purportedly featured what looked like nails penetrating hands and feet. Received 'mystical marriage' at age twelve, but also suffered apparent diabolical attacks, one of such violence that she was blinded in her right eye. Said to have lived entirely without food, with the exception of Communion, for twenty years.

BLESSED LUCIA DE NARNI (1476–1544) In 1497 her stigmata were rigorously examined by the Pope's physician, Bernardo de Recanati, and others, on instructions from Pope Alexander VI. A further examination in Rome was ordered the following year. Her wounds were pronounced genuine, and noted for their sweet-smelling perfume.

BLESSED CATHERINE RACCONIGI (1486–1557) Born Catherine de Matholis, the daughter of a poor manual worker. Received stigmata at the age of twenty-four, her garments becoming soaked in blood, but the wounds later disappeared in answer to her prayers.

ST TERESA OF AVILA (1515–82) Not a stigmatic in the normal sense, but claimed mystic moment when she felt her heart pierced by a spear-carrying angel. At her death her heart was said to have been found with a fissure consistent with this description.

ST CATHERINE DEI RICCI (1522–90) Born Alessandra Lucrezia Romola, she entered the Dominican order at the age of thirteen, becoming professed the following year. Over a period of several years went into weekly ecstasies lasting precisely twenty-eight hours, from noon Thursday until 4 p.m. Friday. Featured right shoulder scar from apparent carrying of the cross. Beatified 1732 and canonised 1746.

DELICIA DI GIOVANNI (1550–c. 1622) Born in Palermo, Sicily. Became Dominican nun at the age of seventeen, and did not begin to receive stigmata until c. 1615, when she was sixty-five. The first sign was merely a wound in her right hand. There followed year by year the left hand, the right foot, the left foot, the wound in the side, wounds as from scourging, and finally, in the last year of her life, wounds as from a crown of thorns.

MARIA DE LA VISITACION (1556–?) Spanish Dominican nun who became prioress of her convent at only twenty-six. Accusations of faking stigmata initially dismissed by doctors in 1587, then renewed, resulting in her being sentenced by the Inquisition to perpetual seclusion.

FRANCESCA DE SERRONE (1557–1600) Born at San Severino della Marche, in the Potenza valley, just north of Tolentino in southern Italy, Francesca received wound in the side at the age of fourteen, by which time she had already become a Franciscan tertiary. She later joined an enclosed convent. The wound in the side would bleed every Friday, and was reported to have the perfume of violets, and to be so hot that it could crack some vessels in which it was collected.

VEN. PASSITEA CROGI (1564–?) Capuchin nun of Siena. Fell into an ecstasy on Palm Sunday 1589, then seemed as if dead until between two and three o'clock on the Good Friday, when she suddenly rose up with a cry, then collapsed again. Blood was seen to pour from her hands, feet, left side (which was reportedly pierced in three places) and head. On being questioned, described vision of Christ crucified, livid and bruised, and covered with wounds streaming with red blood. All medications failed to help her wounds to heal, although they were comparatively superficial. Four years later, on the Wednesday before Good Friday, she received a further vision, accompanied by a thunderclap noise, as a result of which her wounds reopened, this time much deeper than before, her hands and feet reportedly penetrated right through. Bleedings from these, accompanied by severe pain, were mainly at Easter and on other special days, including the feast of St Francis's stigmatisation. Sealed phials of blood collected from her stigmatic wounds have been preserved, and are said on certain occasions to reliquefy. The wounds reportedly continued visible up to her death.

ST MARIA MADDALENA DE' PAZZI (1566–1607) Born Caterina de' Pazzi, of a famous aristocratic Florentine family. Carmelite nun with classic tendency to self-torture, rolling herself in thorn bushes, and lashing herself with nettles and whips. Stigmatised at age nineteen. Said to have eaten and drunk nothing aside from Holy Communion.

ONOFRIO OF FIAMENGA (1566–1639) Franciscan stigmatic. Wound in right side said to have been still open and deep when tomb was opened fourteen years after his death.

LOUISE DE JÉSUS (1569–1628). In early life Madame Jourdain, became Carmelite of Dôle in eastern France, and received stigmatic crown of thorns six months before her death. When she was ill the sisters of the convent infirmary, changing Louise's head-dress, noted her forehead to be pierced and torn, with blood trickling from her wounds onto the pillow.

PUDENZIA ZAGNONI (1583–1650) Joined Franciscan order as Poor Clare nun at the age of twenty. Reputedly feigned madness in order to make herself an object of ridicule. Became stigmatised at the age of sixty-five, two years before her death.

The Seventeenth Century

SUOR MARIA VILLANI, O.P. (1584–1670) Neapolitan Dominicaness whose three confessors, in signed depositions dated 12 and 19 November 1620 and 29 March 1621, attested that they had seen and touched wound in her side. Under protest Suor Maria subsequently showed it to Dona Margarita d'Aragon, Princess of Bisignano, after which the wound disappeared and was not seen again throughout the rest of her life. It appears to have been her only stigmatic manifestation.

MARIA BENIGNA PEPE, (1590–1658) Born at Trapani. Entered Dominican order. On her death was found on her left shoulder, as if branded, a cross surmounted by a crown of thorns.

MOTHER AGNES OF JESUS (1602–1634) Cutler's daughter from Le Puy in the Haute Loire region of southern France, south-west of Lyon. Experienced visions and ecstasies from the age of seven, and received stigmata c. 1614, when she was only twelve. Became Dominican tertiary at the age of nineteen. Said to have diffused 'celestial perfume' and to have been responsible for some miracle cures. Died October 1634 aged approximately thirty-three years.

SOEUR JEANNE DES ANGES (1602–1665). Not strictly a stigmatic, but exhibited stigmatic-type skin-lettering. Born into an aristocratic French family, the daughter of Louis de Belciel, Baron de Coze and his wife Charlotte. From birth she suffered a deformity which gave her a dwarfish physique, and was troublesome in her childhood (to the extent that she was sent away from home), but joined the Ursuline order of nuns, and appeared to improve markedly on becoming transferred to the Order's new convent at Loudun, south-west of Tours. In 1627 she became the convent's Prioress, but soon developed such a love-hate infatuation for Loudun's parson, Urbain Grandier, that she and her nuns affected the most extreme forms of diabolic possession, resulting in Grandier being tried, tortured and burnt at the stake in 1634. Grandier's death failed to check Jeanne and her nuns' possession, which continued for another four years until Jesuit exorcist Jean-Joseph Surin succeeded, but only at the expense of twenty years of his own mental health. Upon one of the apparent devils leaving Jeanne, a cross appeared on her forehead for three weeks. Upon the expulsion of another, the word 'Joseph' appeared imprinted on her left hand, followed by the names of Jesus, Mary and François de Sales, all of which irregularly faded and reappeared up until St John's Day 1662. During the late 1630s Jeanne went on tour, the lettering on her hand being examined by the King and Queen of France, Cardinal Richelieu, Duc Gaston d'Orléans and other dignitaries, and exhibited to huge crowds in Paris, Lyon and elsewhere. Other phenomena included phantom swelling of her abdomen and breasts, as from pregnancy, and gross swelling and blackening of her tongue during 'diabolic' states.

JOANNA MARIA DELLA CROCE (1603–1673) Poor Clare of Rovereto in the Italian Tyrol. Received five wounds and crown of thorns. Wound in the side said to have been visible when her reputedly still incorrupt body was exhumed many years after her death.

ARCHANGELA TARDERA Physician's daughter from Piazza, Sicily. Of the Third Order of St Francis. Fully stigmatised. In 1608, during a spell of blindness, fell into a trance, during which she was found to be covered with contusions and weals.

MARIE MARGUERITE OF THE ANGELS (1605–?) Born in Antwerp in the Valckenissen family. Received stigmata, also accredited with bilocation and prophecy.

ANGELA DELLA PACE (1610–1662) Born in Lauro, Angela was first stigmatised at the age of nine, almost the youngest on record (see Madeleine Morice, b. 1736). The wound in her side was said to give out not only blood, but water so hot that it scalded the hands of those who touched it. Angela became a Dominican tertiary, and became prey to various supranormal events, including mystical marriage with a ring, exchange of the heart, and diabolical attacks.

MARGUERITE PARIGOT/MARGUERITE OF THE BLESSED SACRAMENT (1619–1648) Born at Beaune in the Burgundy region of France, February 1619, she entered the Carmelite order at the age of twelve, and received stigmata a year later. Relived scenes of the Passion, but also became prey to such devastating apparent diabolic attacks that doctors cauterised and even trepanned her skull. Anne of Austria claimed that it was through Marguerite's intercession that she gave birth to the future Louis XIV.

MARIE OCK (1622–84) A working woman of Liège, Belgium. Very poor and sickly, she manifested the lance wound in her right side. She frequently experienced ecstasies combined with apparent torments by devils.

GIOVANNA MARIA BONOMI (d. 1607?) Flesh of her hands said to have stood out like the head of a nail.

ST VERONICA GIULIANI (c. 1640–1727) Nun of the strict walled monastery of Citta di Castello. Was prey to repeated ecstasies, receiving stigmata in hands, feet and side 5 April 1697. These were so rigorously examined by her local bishop, Eustachi, and other superiors, that she prayed they might cease to be visible, but received vision imparting to her that they would last for three years. On 5 April 1700 the hand and foot wounds disappeared, although the wound in the side remained, sometimes bleeding profusely. Wounds would open and bleed on command from her confessor. Subsequently claimed her heart had become imprinted with emblems of the Passion, a phenomenon purportedly verified on the opening up of her body thirty hours after her death.

FATHER JULIAN OF THE CROSS Barefooted Carmelite. Had stigmatic marks like round nail-heads in his feet.

ST MARGARET MARIA ALACOQUE (1647–90) Stigmatic with particularly strong penchant for inflicting injuries upon herself. Habitually bound her body with knotted ropes so tight that they could not be removed without tearing away pieces of her skin. She also apparently burnt or carved the name of Jesus on her breast.

GIROLOMA LOBET (1665–1718) Cutler's daughter, born in Barcelona. Unusual as one of only two stigmatics, among thirty in the eighteenth century, who did not belong to a religious order.

ANNA MARIA CASTRECA (later LA MADRE COSTANTE MARIA) (1670–1736) Born at Fabriano in the Marches of Ancona, Italy, she was taught to read at the age of three by an uncle who terrified her. Both her parents died when she was eight, whereupon she joined the school of a Benedictine convent where two of her aunts were nuns. These in their turn caused her further terrors, as a result of which, shortly after a kind of vision, she suffered a loss of memory, requiring her to learn all over again how to read and to sew, although her original memory returned a year later. About 1688 became unable for a year to eat meat or eggs, only curd and figs. She vomited everything else, and was also observed to bring up blood, balls of hair, bits of string and scraps of paper. Two years later suffered long illness during which she lost all external feeling, and was sometimes unable to stand, although at other times she would hurl herself violently around the room. In 1697, at the age of twenty-six, joined the austere Capuchin order's Fabriano convent, where she quickly manifested serious personality disturbances, including reversion to the speech and manner of a child. These delayed her being allowed to make her vows. Despite these problems, her Fabriano fellow-nuns gradually came to accept her. About the year 1715 she became marked with the stigmata, retaining a permanent wound in her side. Subsequently elected Abbess, an office she held until her death at the age of sixty-six.

The Eighteenth Century

ST MARY FRANCIS OF THE FIVE WOUNDS (?–1791) According to one of her confessors, Don Paschal Nitti, her wounds, which were most developed during Lent, and on Fridays in March, sometimes completely perforated her hands.

MADELEINE MORICE (1736–1769) Born July 1736 at Néant in the diocese of St Malo, Brittany, France. Reportedly stigmatised at the age of eight. Early in adult life she was an impoverished dressmaker, then became schoolmistress, though with little apparent education. Some time during her early years she received the stigmata, losing these for a period, then remanifesting them c. 1768, when she was thirty-two. Also reputedly exhibited bloody sweat when in ecstasy. Lived thirty-three years.

MARIA-JOSEPHA KÜMI (1763–1817) Born at Wollerau, Switzerland. Entered Dominican convent at Wesen near Lake Wallenstadt 1783. Twenty years later received cross-shaped wound in the side, followed by marks of a crown of thorns.

The Nineteenth Century

ANNE CATHARINE EMMERICH (1774–1824) Born of very poor peasant parents, in tiny, run-down hamlet of Flamske, a mile and a half from Coesfeld, Westphalia, West Germany. Became Augustinian nun at Dülmen, also in Westphalia, 1803. After suppression of her convent, stigmatised 1812, inclusive of side wound in form of the Y-shaped crucifix of the church at Coesfeld before which she worshipped as a child. Also featured crown of thorns. Claimed inability to eat food through most of her last years.

MARIA ROSA ANDRIANI (1790–c. 1862) Born at Fracaville, and joined Third Order of Franciscans. Received stigmata in stages, including bleeding from the eyes. Said to have taken no food except Communion for twenty-eight years.

JEANNE BOISSEAU (1797–1872) Daughter of poor French parents from Clisson in the Vendée, Jeanne's life was one series of illnesses and accidents. Stricken by pains of the Passion in 1857, she received profusely bleeding stigmata in 1862 at the age of sixty-five.

THÉRÈSE PUTIGNY (1803–1885) Born at Éply in the Metz region of northeastern France, she suffered ecstasies of reliving scenes from the Passion during which blood flowed from her face like an abundant sweat. She also manifested deep wounds in her side which would disappear with remarkable suddenness, and was prey to purportedly diabolic attacks.

Became lay-sister at the Visitation convent in Metz c. 1825. Was reputed to have powers of bilocation and prophecy.

MADAME MIOLLIS (1806–77) The wife of a joiner of Marseilles, Madame Miollis's stigmata manifested around the year 1840, then gradually disappeared. She was studied by a Dr Reverdit who noted she would sometimes bleed from the hands without any apparent breakage of the skin; at other times she manifested deep wounds, including some resembling the head of a large nail. The manifestations tended to occur on Good Friday or similar penitential days.

VICTOIRE CLAIRE (c. 1808–1883) A humble villager of Coux near Privas, in the Ardèche region of southern France, Victoire was widowed early, after giving birth to several children. Stigmata in her hands and forehead lasted for about fifteen years, and she would lapse into ecstasies in which she was said to remain suspended in the air.

MARIA DE MOERL (1812–1863) Nobleman's daughter born at Caldaro/Kaldern in the Tyrol, Maria's mother died when she was fifteen, leaving her in charge of the female duties for a family of nine. Exceptionally pious, she often lapsed into ecstasy on receiving Communion, and in late autumn 1833 received the five wounds, with bleeding from these on Thursdays and Fridays. Initially she kept these secret, but they became obvious to those who were with her on the Feast of Corpus Christi, 1834, after which she attracted many visitors to Kaldern. Said to have rarely eaten, her only sustenance an occasional morsel of bread and a few grapes. In later life was kept cloistered in Franciscan convent, where she was constantly in ecstasy, as observed by the English visitors Wynne, Pollen and Allies in 1847.

DOMENICA LAZZARI (1815–48) Poor miller's daughter from Capriana in the Italian Tyrol. Bedridden after night of terror 3 June 1833. From development of stigmata in 1834 (which subsequently manifested every week), claimed neither to eat nor drink until her death. Crown of thorns bled on Fridays. Suffered convulsions and beat herself mercilessly with her fists. Hypersensitive to light and other external stimuli. Lived thirty-three years.

CRESCENTIA NIERKLUTSCH (1816–55) Lay stigmatic also from the Tyrol, Crescentia received temporary stigmata, in June 1855, shortly before her death in the same year.

FRANCOISE BARTHEL (1824–1878) Born at Andlau in Alsace. Stigmata studied by Dr Taufflieb of Barr, and by a Strasbourg medical commission.

PALMA MARIA MATARELLI (1825–1888) From Oria near Brindisi, southern Italy. An illiterate peasant girl who married a shepherd, she had three daughters by him, only to lose each in quick succession, followed by her husband, when she was only twenty-eight years old. Four years later, on May 3, 1857, received stigmata which, with exception of wound in the side, mostly disappeared from 1865. Subsequent claimed phenomena included spontaneous fire beneath her clothes, and forehead stigmatic wounds which were sympathetically studied by Dr Imbert-Goubeyre in 1871. As early as 1875 Pope Pius IX told those who questioned him about Palma that investigations by his own officials had shown her to be a fraud, and that he had firm evidence of this in his desk.

ANNIE GIRLING (1827–86) A farmer's daughter born in Little Glemham, Suffolk, England, Annie married a seaman who subsequently became an Ipswich tradesman. At Christmas 1864 she had an ecstatic experience as a result of which she began to believe that she was a new and special incarnation of God, stigmata having appeared in her hands, feet and side. She was the first known English stigmatic, and went on to found a working class religious movement known as the People of God, persuading them that she would not die before the second coming of Christ. The movement, which for a while lived in encampments in the New Forest, disbanded when she died from cancer in 1886.

ISABELLA HENDRICKX (1844–74) From Appels-Termonde, Belgium. Received stigmata fifty days before her death.

TERESA HELENA HIGGINSON (1844–1905) Daughter of a devout Catholic land agent and his Protestant wife, living at Gainsborough, Lincolnshire, in east central England, Teresa was named after Spanish mystic St Teresa of Avila and St Helena, reputed discoverer of the True Cross. During childhood threw herself into sawpit after death of younger brother. As teenager, frequently mortified herself. Frequent illnesses and bouts of fasting. On becoming a teacher near Wigan began ecstatic experiences with further mortifications c. 1874, notably around time Louise Lateau was attracting press attention. Stigmata observed of her that Easter. But in the same year was dismissed from a school in Liscard (Wirral) because of apparent poltergeist phenomena, and in 1877 was accused of stealing £100 from a woman in her lodging house, this money mysteriously being rediscovered after police were called. While living in Bootle during the early 1880s seems to have continued acting out Passion, much to the disturbance and consternation of neighbours. Accusations of drunkenness and other unseemly behaviour seem to have been taken sufficiently seriously that her parish priest and confessor, Father Powell, was moved to another parish, and Teresa subsequently dismissed from her teaching post by his successor.

SISTER MARIE DE JÉSUS CRUCIFIÉ (1846–1879) Carmelite nun based in Bethlehem. In 1868 experienced ecstasy during which she claimed Jesus pierced her heart. Lived thirty-three years. On her death post-mortem surgeon Dr Carpani reported finding a deep triangular lesion in her heart, as if from an old wound.

LOUISE LATEAU (1850–83) Of peasant parentage, Bois d'Haine, Belgium. At age of eleven trodden on by a cow, or gored by a bull (stories differ). Tended sick during Belgian cholera epidemic of 1866. The following year nearly died from attack of angina. On 3 January 1868 began experiencing crucifixion pains, followed by manifestation of wound in the side 24 April, bleeding from upper surface of her feet 1 May, and hands a few weeks later. Bleeding subsequently recurred every Friday, in all some 800 times, until her death. Said to have been able, while in ecstasy, to converse in unlearned languages such as Latin and English. Said to have exhibited dramatic weight changes despite having taken no food apart from Holy Communion after 30 March 1871. Marked increase in her sufferings from 1879. Lived thirty-three years.

MARIE-JULIE JAHENNY (c. 1853–1930s) Breton peasant woman of hamlet of La Fraudais, near Blain (Loire-Inférieure), not far from Nantes. Received wounds in hands, feet and side 21 March 1873, then crown of thorns 5 October, imprint on left shoulder 25 November, dorsal hand and foot wounds 6 December, followed by cord-like wrist-marks and an emblematic pattern over her heart 12 January 1874. Two days later there appeared stripes, as from scourging, on her ankles, legs and forearms, a stigmatic ring 20 February of the same year, and ultimately on her breast the words *O crux ave* together with a cross and a flower, 7 December 1875. These latter were still visible nearly twenty years later. After receiving stigmata began to eat very little food, then in 1874 had two periods of total abstinence, the second of ninety-four days, followed by a claimed abstinence of more than five years from December 18, 1875.

SISTER MARIA DELLA PASSIONE (died 1912) First exhibited crown of thorns wounds Holy Week 1903. Other stigmata followed later in the year, and bled every Friday until her death.

ST GEMMA GALGANI (1878–1903) Born of poor parents at Camigliano in Tuscany. Lived most of her life in Lucca, Italy. Orphaned at nineteen years of age. Prevented by spinal tuberculosis from becoming Passionist nun, but took the three vows privately, with, in addition, a vow of perfection. Frequently prayed before image of scourged Christ. Bound herself tightly with a rope. On a Friday in March 1901 experienced scourging of Christ and was found by her adopted mother to be covered in bloody weals. These apparently reproduced exactly those on her favourite crucifix. Stigmata subsequently appeared each Thursday about 8 pm until 3 pm the next day. Featured wound on left shoulder, as from carrying of the cross. Believed herself to have been occasionally prey to diabolic possession.

The Twentieth Century

PADRE PIO OF PIETRELCINA (1887–1968) Born Francesco Forgione, of peasant parentage, Pietrelcina, southern Italy. Joined ascetic Capuchin order 1902. Frequently ill and emotionally disturbed during immediately subsequent years. In September 1915, the anniversary of St Francis's stigmatisation, while praying complained of stinging pains in hands. Actual wounds, in hands, feet and left side, the latter in the form of an inverted cross, first appeared 20 September 1918. Although repeatedly pained by these, which he carried until his death, Padre Pio was from this point freed from his earlier debilitating illnesses. He spent most of the rest of his life at the monastery of San Giovanni Rotondo, Foggia. Ate extremely frugally, particularly for a man of his size, and needed little sleep.

DOROTHY KERIN (1889–1963) Born in Walworth, London, the daughter of an Irish Catholic father and singer mother, Dorothy's life was uneventful until her father's unexpected death in 1902, when she was only thirteen. She then suffered ten years of illness, the last five of these bedridden, diagnosed in the later stages as incurable tuberculosis. By February 1912 she had taken no solid food for six months, and was deaf, blind and semi-conscious. The evening of 18 February, expecting her to die, sixteen relatives and friends were gathered round her bedside when she stood up and walked steadily across the room, pronouncing herself cured. During the years immediately following she reported various visions of Jesus and the Virgin Mary, followed, on 8 December 1915 by receiving stigmata first in her left hand, then, in the ensuing days, in her right hand, her left side, and her feet. These stayed open for several days and remained visible for several years, temporarily disappearing during a time of depression only to re-manifest, somewhat smaller than before, in 1921. In 1929 Dorothy opened a House of Healing, St Raphael's, in Ealing, London, subsequently finding a more permanent home for this work with the acquisition of the still extant Burrswood Healing Centre, near Groombridge in Kent. Like other stigmatics, she was accredited with some remarkable healings, and apparently paranormal appearances to individuals in need.

BERTHE MRAZEK/GEORGES MARASCO (1890–?) Born Brussels, daughter of loose-living Czechoslovak father and Belgian mother. Early years spent as circus performer and café singer. Gave birth to illegitimate daughter Adele, 1913. Reputedly secret service agent and friend of nurse Edith Cavell, World War I. Ascetic living precipitated serious health breakdown immediately post-war, accompanied by paralysis and blindness. July 1920 claimed miracle cure at shrine of Notre Dame of Hal, followed by reception of stigmata, including crown of thorns and wound in side. Wounds photographed 1922, 1923, but doubts began to be expressed and late in 1924 she was arrested for obtaining money by deception and committed to an asylum as insane.

THERESE NEUMANN (1898–1962) Born between Good Friday and Easter Saturday, 1898, at Konnersreuth, Bavaria, the eldest daughter of a poor tailor. As teenager alleged to have been twice victim of attempted rapes. Serious spinal and head injuries, accompanied by paralysis, as a result of accidents 1918. Blindness and convulsions 1919. Eyesight restored day of beatification of St Therese of Lisieux, 29 April 1923, followed by restoration of mobility day of St Therese's canonisation, 17 May 1925. Vision of Jesus and onset of wound in side 4 March 1926. Bleeding from all wounds, including shoulders and knees, would occur on Fridays, mainly during Lent. During visions, claimed to hear and reproduce Aramaic spoken by Jesus. From Christmas 1926 until the end of her life, said to have neither eaten nor drunk anything except daily Communion, although after a fifteen-day observation of her every activity July 1927, during which never less than two nuns were with her at all times, her father refused to allow her to be subjected to any further intensive examination. Suffered apparent stroke, with paralysis of whole right side of her body, early July 1940. Apparently miraculously cured a few days later by vision of the Assumption of Mary. With her confessor, Father Naber, received into the Third Order of St Francis 3 September 1946.

ELENA AJELLO (b. 1901) From Calabria. Exhibited bloody tears and sweat at age of twenty-two. Appears to have identified herself with St Rita of Cascia.

ELIZABETH K. (1902–?) Born in southern Germany in family with history of neurosis. Somnambulistic as child. Mother died when Elizabeth was six. Imaginative and intelligent at school, but began suffering from shaking limbs, headaches, and then right body paralysis, culminating in numbness, inability to eat and speak, and bladder and bowel disfunctions. Hypnotic, electrical and psychiatric treatments produced only temporary relief, as a result of which in 1929 psychiatrist Dr Albert Lechler, of Elberfeld, decided to employ her as a servant in his own home. He noted her tendency to take on the pains and illnesses of others, but most particularly her reactions after viewing a slide show with scenes of Jesus's crucifixion, Easter 1932, when she complained of severe pains in her hands and feet. On hypnotising Elizabeth and redirecting her concentration on hand and foot nailing she began to exhibit nail wounds in hands and feet, then, on further suggestion, to cry blood-stained tears, and to bleed from an apparent crown of thorns. Could gain weight while living on little or no food, and required only two to four hours sleep.

HERR ARTHUR OTTO M. (1902–?) Born in Hagenau, Alsatia. Family lived in and near Hamburg from 1906, Arthur becoming in adult life a well-to-do Protestant timber merchant of the Hamburg suburb of Berne. In May 1928 suffered a car accident, after which he had some experiences of an undetermined nature, followed from 1935 by wounds of crown of thorns, which would appear three or four times a year, then later more frequently, at four- or six-weekly intervals, accompanied by stigmata in the hands, feet and side. In 1943 an air-raid bomb flung him down a high staircase, after which he began to manifest a distinct cross on his forehead. The onset of the stigmata would be preceded by strong pressure on both sides of the head, and intense headache – in his own words: 'I feel like having lead in my head' – these pains disappearing once the wounds, usually accompanied by a vision of Jesus, began to open. Herr Arthur also sometimes suffered loss of hearing and vision during such occurences, together with serious personality disorientation and weight loss. Arthur was reported to have had no special religious inclinations, being only nominally Protestant and never attending church.

MRS EVA McISAAC (1902–) Part Indian housewife, born Eva Baye in the tiny (200 pop.) village of Uptergrove between Lakes Simcoe and Couchiching, eighty-six miles north of Toronto, Ontario, Canada. Roman Catholic parentage. Married Uptergrove farmer Donald, giving birth to eight children, of whom two died. In 1937 experienced vision, accompanied by small painful sore on the back of right hand. During next three years began exhibiting further wounds in hands, feet, left side, head, back and right shoulder. Pain and bleeding gradually became concentrated to between 6 and 9 Friday evenings, accompanied by terrifying agonies.

'MRS H.' [Australian psychiatric patient] (1909–1963) Born in Poland. Unloved by parents. Pregnant at sixteen and unwittingly bigamously married to child's father, who later committed suicide. Forced labour camps Germany 1941–5. Emigrated to Australia 1949, becoming Sunday School teacher, but refused entry to religious order 1956. Room resembled chapel, with pride of place to picture of Veronica's Veil. Hospitalised after spider bite 1958, when upper arms noted to be insensitive to pain. In same year patient at Brisbane Mental Hospital where on 23 May she claimed vision of Virgin Mary, subsequently every Friday around 11 am entering trance during which she wept tears stained with blood. At home she would bleed from her eyelids around 4.45 pm on Fridays, attracting local Catholics to come to her garden with flowers. Predicted she would die on a Friday in November. In fact died on Saturday 16 November 1963, apparently from an overdose of barbiturates.

SUOR TOMASSINA POSSI (1911–1945) Dominican nun of the convent of Sondrio, in the Italian Alps close to the border between Italy and Switzerland. Received nail-wounds in hands and feet, and wound in the side. Thirty-four years old at death.

146

ETHEL CHAPMAN (1921–1980) Born at midnight Whit Sunday 1921. Anglican religious background. Father died of World War I injuries while Ethel was still young. Became stage entertainer. Married for two years to a man whom she discovered to be a bigamist with four children. Around this time onset of first symptoms of multiple sclerosis. Started writing poetry 1974. At Easter this same year, while seriously ill, and after reading about the Crucifixion in an illustrated Bible, began feeling crucifixion pains, subsequently exhibiting bleeding from centre of palms.

SALVATORE MARCHESE (c. 1922–) One-time hospital caretaker from Catania in Sicily, wounds have appeared on his hands since 1970.

BROTHER GINO BURRESI (1932–) Born at Gambassi, near Florence, and not ordained a priest until he was fifty-one. Publicity-shy, but accredited with wounds of the nails in his wrists (as per the Shroud of Turin), not in his palms. Now lives near Rome.

GIGLIOLA GIORGINI (1933–) Since the early 1960s has lived in Baronto, Pistoia, to the north-west of Florence. Stigmata take the form of violet-coloured linear scars in her hands. Her authenticity strongly disclaimed by the ecclesiastical authorities. In 1984 convicted of fraud by Italian court, amid considerable publicity.

TERESA MUSCO (1943–76) Poor Italian seamstress, stigmatised in a vision in 1969. Although purportedly illiterate, during her trances she would speak what was claimed to be Aramaic, or write out whole passages from the Bible. She predicted she would die at the same age as Jesus. Lived thirty-three years.

JANE HUNT (1957–) Daughter of Catholic Derbyshire coal-miner and Anglican mother. Deaf until age six, yet aware of Christ from as early as she can remember. After limited schooling began working in a factory at fourteen before getting married three years later. Chose to attend Anglican church. Suffered series of tragic miscarriages. Has experienced several visions. On 25 July (St James's Day) 1985, received stigmata to her hands, which remained until operation for hysterectomy 1987. Claims to have been able to heal certain individuals during services at her local church.

VERA D'AGOSTINO (1959–) Italian working man's daughter, born 21 February 1959 at Moscufo in the province of Pescara. In 1968 family moved to Chieti, a few miles to the south of Pescara. In 1979 received vision of Jesus, followed by stigmatic wound in the side, also the hands, then the covering of her body with bloody weals as from a scourging. In 1979 left the family home, becoming in February the following year a missionary sister of the Congregation of the Sacred Hearts of Jesus

Stigmata

and Mary at Chieti. In 1982 said to have cured forty-two year old Maria Emanuele of multiple sclerosis.

CLORETTA ROBINSON (1962–) Black Baptist girl from West Oakland, California. Bleeding from palm of left hand began in school classroom 17 March 1972, after having read John Webster's *Crossroads*, a religious book about the Crucifixion, approximately one week before. Intermittently stigmatised in her hands, feet and forehead, during the next nineteen days up to and including Good Friday.

ROBERTO CASARIN (1963–) Originating from Riese, Treviso, to the north of Venice, subsequently moving to Turin. In 1981 mysterious happenings accompanied his prayers to the Virgin Mary. In 1982 Cardinal Ballestrero of Turin denied any genuine supernatural phenomena associated with Roberto, but on Good Friday 1983 a bloody cross manifested on his forehead. Some in Italy have labelled him the new Padre Pio.

NOTES AND REFERENCES

Chapter 1

1 Interview by the author recorded with Jane Hunt at her home 8 November 1987.
2 *Just Jane,* transmitted on the ITV network 2 pm, Sunday 5 October 1986.
3 From *Just Jane,* as above.
4 Interview with Gordon in *Just Jane,* as above.
5 Quoted without original source in René Biot *The Riddle of the Stigmata,* London, Burns and Oates 1962, p. 40.
6 Quoted without original source in Rev Charles M. Carty *Padre Pio the Stigmatist,* Dublin, Clonmore and Reynolds, 1955.
7 Norman St John Stevens 'Why the Holy Shroud and Padre Pio make me smile', *Catholic Herald,* 12 May 1978.
8 See particularly the photographs published in Carty, op. cit., all these quoted as the copyright of Abresch Federico of San Giovanni Rotondo, Foggia, Italy.
9 Quoted, with accompanying photos, in Carty, op. cit., pp. 111, 112. Although all the cases are anecdotal, Carty provides a detailed list of Padre Pio's alleged cures.
10 *Acta Apostolicae Sedis,* 5 July 1923, p. 356.
11 Ibid, 1926, 18, 186.
12 Ibid, 1931, 23, 233.
13 A. Imbert-Goubeyre, *La Stigmatisation, l'ecstase divine, les miracles de Lourdes, réponse aux libres penseurs,* 2 vols, Clermont, Bellet, 1894.

Chapter 2

1   *Fioretti* as translated in *The Little Flowers of Saint Francis*, trans. L. Sherley-Price, Harmondsworth Penguin, 1959, p. 165.
2   Ibid, p. 167.
3   Translated from the Latin of the parchment preserved in the Convent of Friars Minor, Assisi.
4   Translated from Reginald Balfour *Seraphic Keepsake*, p. 38, as quoted in Thurston *The Physical Phenomena of Mysticism*, London, Burns Oates, 1952, p. 44.
5   Brother Masseo, source not noted.
6   Thomas of Celano *Prima Vita*, trans. A. G. Ferrers Howell, ii, §§94–95, ed. Eduardus d'Alençon, Rome, 1906.
7   N. H. J. Westlake, F.S.A., *The Authentic Portraiture of St Francis of Assisi*. The first of the paintings, by Pisano, is dated to 1230.
8   Westlake, op. cit., p. 16.
9   Francis's speech, as quoted in translation in Lord Longford's *Francis of Assisi, A Life for All Seasons*, London, Weidenfeld, 1978, p. 14, with slight modernisation.
10 Quoted without original source in Edward F. Hartung, 'St Francis and Medieval Medicine', *Annals of Medical History*, 7, 1935, p. 85.
11 Hartung, op. cit.
12 St Bonaventure, *Legenda Major*, xiv 2, as trans. E. Gurney Salter, London, 1910.
13 *Annals of Dunstable* (Rolls series, ed. Luard), p. 76.
14 *Annales de Oseneia* (Rolls series, ed. Luard), p. 63.
15 Capgrave. Rolls series, Ed., p. 151, quoted in Thurston, *Physical Phenomena*, op. cit., p. 37.

Chapter 3

1   *Acta Sanctorum*, March, vol III, p. 751, as translated in Thurston, *Physical Phenomena*, p. 39.
2   Quoted in translation in Montague Summers, *The Physical Phenomena of Mysticism*, London, Rider, 1950, p. 157.
3   The full text is published by the Bollandists (Jesuit editors of the *Santa Sanctorum*), in their Catalogue of the Hagiographical MSS. of Brussels, col I, pp. 362–378.
4   Ibid, §4, p. 365.
5   Thurston, op. cit., pp. 40, 41.
6   *Analecta Bollandiana* (Bollandists' quarterly review), vol XVIII, pp. 315–316.
7   'ne' luoghi più segreti della casa', V. Puccini, *Vita della Ven, Madre Suor Maria Madalena de' Pazzi*, Napoli, 1652, p. 3. For this and other

material on Maria Maddalena de' Pazzi I am indebted to the chapter about her in Eric Dingwall's *Very Peculiar People*, Rider and Co., 1950.

8 L.Grimes, *Esprit des Saints Illustres*, 6 vols, Paris, 1845–1846, vi, p. 306.

9 Dingwall, op. cit., p. 131.

10 Horatio Brown (ed.), *Calendar of State Papers; Venice*, quoted in Thurston, op. cit., p. 85.

11 Aldous Huxley, *The Devils of Loudun*, London, Chatto and Windus, 1952.

12 Thomas Killigrew, Letter in *European Magazine*, February 1803.

13 Huxley, op. cit., p. 292.

14 Soeur Jeanne des Anges, *Autobiographie d'une hystérique possédée*, ed., with introduction and notes, Drs Gabriel Legué and Gilles de la Tourette, Paris, 1886.

Chapter 4

1 Quoted, with original source, in Summers, *The Physical Phenomena of Mysticism*, p. 163.

2 To Brentano's original assiduousness we owe the remarkable *The Life of Jesus Christ and Biblical Revelations, from the visions of the Venerable Anne Catherine Emmerich as recorded in the journals of Clemens Brentano*, arranged and edited by the Very Rev Carl E.Schmoger, 4 vols, New York, Sentinel Press, 1914.

3 W.T.Allies, *Journal in France in 1845 and 1846 with letters from Italy in 1847*, Brussels, J.B.De Mortier, 1850.

4 Dr L.Dei Cloche, 'Annotaziano intorno', *Annales de médicine universelle*, Milan, November 1837, quoted in translation in Thurston, *Physical Phenomena of Mysticism*, pp. 76–77.

5 Allies, op. cit., pp. 134–135.

6 Ibid.

7 Dr Lefebvre, *Louise Lateau de Bois d'Haine, ses extases, ses stigmates*, de Lannoy, Brussels, 1920, quoted in translation in Biot, op. cit., p. 33.

8 Ibid, p. 107.

9 Ibid, pp. 107–108.

10 This and the succeeding passages, ibid, pp. 108–110.

11 Dr Imbert-Goubeyre *La Stigmatisation*, vol II, p. 27, as translated in Thurston, op. cit., p. 64.

12 Dr Imbert-Goubeyre *La Stigmatisation*, vol I, p. 567 as translated in Thurston, op. cit., pp. 78–79.

13 Mgr Barbier de Montault, *Oeuvres Complètes*, vol 5, 1892, pp. 197–199, as translated in Thurston, op. cit., pp. 81–82.

Chapter 5

1 As translated from the French in Herbert Thurston 'The Extraordinary Case of Georges Marasco', *The Month*, no. 726, December 1924, p. 495. Thurston's spelling 'Hal' has been updated to the modern 'Halle'.
2 Herbert Thurston, continuation of the above article in *The Month* no. 727 of 25 January 1925.
3 Ibid, p. 55.
4 Ibid.
5 Thurston, as note 1, p. 499.
6 *La Nation Belge*, 3 December 1924, as translated in the second of Thurston's articles, p. 53.
7 The main details of Therese Neumann's life have been principally derived from the following biographies available in English: Johannes Steiner, *Therese Neumann, a portrait based on authentic accounts, journals and documents*, New York, Alba House, 1967; and Anni Spiegl, *The life and death of Therese Neumann of Konnersreuth*, Eichstatt, 1973.
8 Frederick von Lama *Therese Neuman, a stigmatist of our days*, trans. A.P.Schimberg, Bruce, Milwaukee, 1929.
9 As published in Dr Boreslias de Poray Madeyski, *Le cas de la visionnaire stigmatisée Thérèse Neumann de Konnersreuth, étude analytique et critique du problème*, Paris, Lethielleux, 1940, quoted in translation in Hilda C.Graef, *The Case of Therese Neumann*, Cork, Mercier, 1950, p. 60 ff.
10 Ibid, p. 63.
11 Poray Madeyski, op. cit., as quoted in translation in Biot, op. cit., pp. 104–105.
12 Dorothy Musgrave Arnold *Dorothy Kerin, Called by Christ to Heal*, London, Hodder and Stoughton, 1965, p. 36. For further information on Dorothy Kerin, see also Monica Furlong's *Burrswood, Focus of Healing*, London, Hodder and Stoughton, 1978, and Johanna Ernest *The Teaching of Dorothy Kerin*, private publication c. 1975.
13 Quoted in Frank Hamilton 'A Miracle at Uptergrove?', *MacLean's Magazine*, 15 September 1950.
14 Ibid.
15 Ibid.
16 F.A.Whitlock and J.V.Hynes 'Religious stigmatisation: an historical and psychophysiological enquiry', *Psychological Medicine*, 1978, 8, pp. 185–202.
17 Ibid, p. 191–192.

18 Laretta F.Early and Joseph E.Lifschutz, 'A Case of Stigmata', *Archives of General Psychiatry*, 30 February 1974, pp. 197–200.
19 Ted Harrison, *The Marks of the Cross*, London, Darton, Longman and Todd, 1981, pp. 32, 33.
20 Harrison, op. cit., p. 75.

Chapter 6

1 John 20: 25, *Jerusalem Bible* translation. In the original Greek the word for 'hand' included the wrist.
2 See Dr Pierre Barbet, *The Passion of Our Lord Jesus Christ*, trans. the Earl of Wicklow, Dublin, Clonmore and Reynolds, 1954, chapter 5.
3 In 1968 the only known remains of a crucifixion victim were discovered in a New Testament period Jewish cemetery in north Jerusalem. A pronounced scratch to the wrist-end of the radius bone was interpreted as indicating wrist-nailing. See Nicu Haas, 'Anthropological Observations on the Skeletal Remains from Giv'at ha-Mivtar', *Israel Exploration Journal* 20, 1970.
4 *The Little Flowers of St Francis*, op. cit., p. 167.
5 Gerald Molloy, *A Visit to Louise Lateau*, London, 1873, p. 26.
6 Padre Germano, *Life of Gemma Galgani*, trans. A.M.O'Sullivan, London, Sands, 1914, p. 85.
7 Whitlock and Hynes, 'Religious stigmatisation', op. cit., p. 191.
8 Early and Lifschutz 'A Case of Stigmata', op. cit., p. 199.
9 Personal interview with Jane Hunt.
10 From Dr Lefebvre, *Louise Lateau de Bois d'Haine, ses extases, ses stigmates*, as translated in Biot, op. cit., p. 33.
11 Padre Germano *Life of Gemma Galgani*, trans. A.M.O'Sullivan, Sands and Co., p. 62.
12 Personal interview with Jane Hunt.
13 Process, *Novissima Positio super Virtutibus Responsio*, p. 78, as translated in Thurston, *Physical Phenomena*, op. cit., p. 56.
14 Padre Germano, op. cit., p. 62.
15 Quoted without original source in Biot, op. cit., p. 41.
16 Quoted without original source in Carty, *Padre Pio*, op. cit., p. 190.
17 *The Little Flowers of St Francis*, op. cit., pp. 166–167.
18 N.H.J.Westlake, *The Authentic Portraiture of St Francis of Assisi*.
19 Ibid, p. 16 (quoted without source).
20 S.Bonaventurae, *Opera*, ed. Quaracchi, vol VIII, p. 576, as translated in Thurston, *Physical Phenomena*, op. cit., p. 48.
21 Thurston, op. cit., p. 56.
22 *Letter of the Earl of Shrewsbury*, London, 1842, p. 57.
23 As note 11.
24 Dorothy Arnold *Dorothy Kerin . . .*, op. cit., p. 37.

25 Dr Louis of Versailles, *La semaine sainte de 1930 à Konnersreuth*, as translated in Biot, op. cit., p. 39.
26 Ibid.
27 Anni Spiegl *Life and Death of Therese Neumann*, op. cit., photo opposite p. 49.
28 Dr Imbert-Goubeyre, *La Stigmatisation*, op. cit.
29 Thurston, op. cit., p. 67, after Pizzicaria *Un Tesoro Nascoto, osia diario de S. Veronica Giuliani* I, (1895), pp. 288–289.

Chapter 7

1 Catherine Emmerich, quoted in Summers, *Physical Phenomena*, p. 163.
2 Ibid, p. 165.
3 Ted Harrison, *The Marks of the Cross*, op. cit., pp. 29, 30.
4 L.Grimes, *Esprit des saints illustres*, 6 vols, Paris, 1845–1846, vi, p. 306, as translated by Dingwall.
5 Lady Cecil Kerr, *Teresa Higginson*, 1928, pp. 73–75.
6 Friedrich von Lama, *Further Chronicles of Therese Neumann*, trans. A.P.Schimberg, Milwaukee, Bruce, 1932.
7 Anni Spiegl *Life and Death of Therese Neumann of Konnersreuth*, pp. 46–47 and 59–60.
8 Anne Catherine Emmerich *The Life of Jesus Christ and Biblical Revelations*, arr. and edited Revd Carl E.Schmöger, New York, Sentinel Press, 1914.
9 The account of a priest eyewitness, sent to Ritter von Lama, and quoted in Thurston, *Physical Phenomena, op. cit.*, p. 113.
10 Ibid, note 2.
11 Johannes Steiner, *Therese Neumann*, op. cit., p. 53.
12 Quoted in J.Teodorowicz, *Mystical Phenomena in the Life of Therese Neumann*, Eng. trans. 1947, p. 479.
13 Ian Wilson, *Reincarnation?*, Harmondsworth, Penguin, 1982; also *The After Death Experience*, London, Sidgwick and Jackson, 1987.
14 Whitlock and Hynes, op. cit., p. 191.
15 Ted Harrison, op. cit. p. 29.
16 Early and Lifschutz, op. cit., p. 199.
17 Interview with Jane Hunt.
18 See, for instance, the fresco of the Deposition from the Church at Nerezi, Yugoslavia, dated to 1164.

Chapter 8

1 Quoted in Biot, op. cit., p. 120.
2 Corbett Thigpen and Hervey Cleckley, *The Three Faces of Eve*, London, Secker and Warburg, 1957.

3 Chris Sizemore and Elen Pittillo, *Eve*, London, Gollancz, 1978.
4 Daniel Keyes, *The Minds of Billy Milligan*, New York, Random House, 1981.
5 Flora Rheta Schreiber, *Sybil*, Harmondsworth, Penguin, 1975.
6 Sizemore and Pittillo, op. cit., p. 432.
7 For her biography, see Buti, *Vita della Madre Costante Maria Castreca*. A good summary appears in Thurston, *Physical Phenomena*, op. cit., pp. 104–109.
8 Ibid, p. 66, as translated in Thurston, p. 108.
9 Friedrich von Lama, *Therese Neumann, a stigmatic of our time*, trans. A.P.Schimberg, Milwaukee, Bruce, 1929.
10 Sizemore and Pittillo, op. cit., p. 255.
11 See Thurston, op. cit., p. 114.
12 Quoted in Richard Whitting, 'Saint or Sinner?' *Liverpool Echo*, 11 May 1972.
13 Rev Charles Carty, *Padre Pio the Stigmatist*, op. cit., p. 16.
14 Anni Spiegl, *The Life and Death of Therese Neumann*, op. cit., pp. 59–60.
15 From Brother Leo, *Speculum Perfectionis*, ed. Paul Sabatier, 1928, p. 115, as quoted in E.Hartung, 'St Francis and Medieval Medicine', *Annals of Medical History*, 7, 1935, pp. 87, 88.
16 Carty, op. cit., pp. 192–197.
17 *Relation* of S.Veronica Giuliani, as quoted in Pizzicaria, *Un Tesoro Nascoto, ossia diario di S.Veronica Giuliani*, 1895, I, pp. 288–289, as translated in Thurston, *Physical Phenomena*, p. 67.

Chapter 9

1 T.X.Barber, *Hypnosis: A Scientific Approach*, New York, Van Nostrand Reinhold, 1969.
2 Gordon L.Paul, 'The Production of Blisters by Hypnotic Suggestion: Another Look', *Psychosomatic Medicine*, vol 25, no. 3, 1963, pp. 233–244.
3 'Dermographia' entry in *Concise Home Doctor*, Amalgamated Press Ltd, 2 vols, 1938.
4 See Peter Moss with Joe Keeton, *Encounters with the Past: How Man Can Experience and Relive History*, Sidgwick and Jackson, 1979.
5 Information from Joe Keeton.
6 Information provided by Joe Keeton. A dramatised documentary of the Kitty Jay regression was produced by Westward Television during 1980.
7 Alfred Lechler, *Das Rätsel von Konnersreuth in Lichte eines neuer Falles von Stigmatisation*, Elberfeld, 1933.
8 English translation from the above kindly provided for the author by Mrs Iris Sampson.

9   Ibid.
10 Ibid.
11 Dr Robert Moody, 'Bodily Changes During Abreaction', *The Lancet*, vol II, 28 December 1946, p. 934.
12 Second paper by Dr Robert Moody in *The Lancet*, vol I, June 1948, p. 964.

Chapter 10

1   A.I.Spiridovich, *Raspoutine*, 1863–1916, Paris, 1935, p. 71, as translated Alex de Jonge, *The Life and Times of Grigorii Rasputin*, Collins, 1982.
2   D.P.Agle, 'Psychological factors in haemophilia', *Annals of the New York Academy of Science*, 240, pp. 221–225.
3   *The Little Flowers of St Francis*, op. cit., pp. 166–167.
4   Thurston, *Physical Phenomena*, op. cit., p. 50.
5   Ibid, p. 49.
6   Dorothy Arnold, *Dorothy Kerin*, op. cit., p. 37.
7   Dr Richard Dreaper, 'Recalcitrant Warts on the Hand Cured by Hypnosis', *The Practitioner*, February 1978, vol 220, pp. 305–310.
8   Dr A.A.Mason, 'A Case of Congenital Ichthyosiform Erythrodermia of Brocq Treated by Hypnosis', *British Medical Journal*, 23 August 1952, pp. 422–423.
9   Ibid.
10 R.D.Willard, 'Breast Enlargement through Visual Imagery and Hypnosis', *American Journal of Clinical Hyponosis*, 1977, 19 (4), p. 195.
11 Dr O.Carl Simonton, Stephanie Matthews-Simonton and James L.Creighton, *Getting Well Again*, Bantam Books, 1978.
12 Ibid, pp. 144–145.
13 Ibid, pp. 20–21.

Chapter 11

1   Thomas Killigrew, Letter in *European Magazine*, February 1803.
2   *Compendio della Vita della B.Stefana Quinzani*, Parma, 1784, p. 60, translated Thurston, *Physical Phenomena*, op. cit., p. 201.
3   *Vita e Dottrina di Santa Catarina da Genoa*, ed. 1847, p. 168, as quoted in Thurston, op. cit., p. 202.
4   Dr Imbert-Goubeyre, *La Stigmatisation*, vol II, pp. 131–136.
5   W.T.Allies, *Journal in France in 1845 and 1848 with letters from Italy in 1847*, Brussels, J.B.De Mortier, 1850.
6   Alfred Lechler, op. cit.
7   Dr Imbert-Goubeyre, as quoted in Biot, op. cit., pp. 61–80.
8   Canon A.Thiéry, *Nouvelle Biographie de Louise Lateau d'après les documents authentiques*, vol 2, p. 413, quoted and translated in Thurston, p. 350.

9   Dr Warlomont, as referred to in O.D.Ratnoff, 'Stigmata: Where mind and body meet, a study of autoerythrocyte sensitisation', *Medical Times*, 97, pp. 155, 156.
10 Poray-Madeyski, op. cit., pp. 66–70, as quoted in Biot, p. 64.
11 Ibid, p. 65.
12 Dalbert Hallenstein, 'Saints', *Sunday Times* 9 Nov. 1980.
13 Anni Spiegl, op. cit., p. 51.
14 Charles Carty, op. cit., p. 23.
15 Alfred Lechler, op. cit.
16 Ted Harrison, *The Marks of the Cross*, op. cit., p. 54.
17 Ibid.
18 Interview with the author, 8 November 1987.
19 A.M.O'Sullivan, *Teresa Higginson, Servant of God*, quoted in Summers, op. cit., p. 61.
20 Johannes Steiner, *Therese Neumann*, op. cit., p. 193.
21 John McCaffery, *The Friar of San Giovanni*, London, Darton, Longman and Todd, 1978, pp. 1–3.
22 Ibid, pp. 26–28.
23 B.Laviosa, *Vita di S.M.Maria Francesca delle Cinque Piaghe*, Rome, 1866, p. 86, trans. in Thurston, *Physical Phenomena*, p. 230.
24 Ted Harrison, *The Marks of the Cross*, op. cit., pp. 14, 15.
25 McCaffery, op. cit., p. 7.
26 The reference here is to St Anthony of Padua, who while preaching on Holy Thursday, 1227, in the church of St Pierre du Queriox in Limoges, is said to have remembered that at this very same time he was supposed to be chanting a lesson of Tenebrae among his own community of friars. Breaking off from the lesson, he reportedly put his hood over his head, at that same moment appearing to his own community, where he chanted the lesson on schedule. On finishing this he put back his hood and resumed his sermon in the pulpit in Limoges.
27 Charles Carty, op. cit., p. 55.
28 Father Michael Hollings, *Padre Pio*, documentary of BBC–TV 22 September 1968.

Chapter 12

1   See Bryan Silcock 'The new clues that challenge Darwin, *Sunday Times*, 8 March 1981, p. 13.

INDEX

159

Index

Index

stress: and evolutionary theory 127–8;
  physical/mental, effects of 82–3,
  91–2, 126

Tardera, Archangela 138
Taylor, *Rev* Austen: testimony re
  Dorothy Kerin 55
television reportage: Jane Hunt 4–5;
  self-hypnosis 103
Telyakovsky, V.A.: Rasputin and the
  Tsarevitch 102
Teresa of Avila, *Saint* 135
Thérèse of Lisieux, *Saint*: Therese
  Neumann 48–9
Thomas of Celano: testimony re St
  Francis 13
Three Faces of Eve (book *and* film) 84
Thurston, *Rev* Herbert: Elizabeth of
  Herkenrode and Philip of Clairvaux
  21–2; and case of Mrazek, Bertha
  44–6; *quoted* 77
Turin, Holy Shroud of 63, 64

Uptergrove (Ontario, Canada): Eva
  McIsaac 55

Vanna of Orvieto, *Blessed* 132

Victoria, *Queen of the United Kingdom*:
  and haemophilia 101
Villani, *Suor* Maria, O.P. 137
visions 73–7
visualisation in hypnotic therapy
  107–9

Warlomont, *Dr*: testimony re Louise
  Lateau 38–9, 114
West Oakland (California USA):
  Cloretta Robinson 58–9
Westener, *Dr* Frantz Wilhelm 31–2
Westlake, N.H.J.: *quoted* on painting
  of St Francis 13
Willard, *Dr* R.D.: breast enlargement,
  cosmetic 107
William, *Brother*, of Pershore Abbey:
  testimony re Dorothy Kerin 69, 104
wounds: location of, on body 63–4;
  pathological characteristics 64–71
Wyatt: *Rev* Peter, and Jane Hunt 5
Wykes, Thomas: *quoted* on Council of
  Oxford trial (1222) 18
Wynne, J.H., testimony re Domenica
  Lazzari 33–5, 112

Zagnoni, Pudenzia 137

164